Cover Design
by Marilyn Seidl Sobwick

Invented in the 8th century, the hourglass was used to measure increments of time. This device, often depicted as a symbol, evokes the concept that human existence is fleeting, and that the "sands of time" will run out for every source of life on earth.

This celestial design illustrates our vast universe. Looking up to the cosmos calls our attention to our soulful existence. Pillars of light rays in the backgound represent our ever present God with a single bright light illuminating to let us know He'll lead us to eternity.

Each story claims reference to time and a necessary connection made with the eternal advisor. Thus, our eternal X change.

what if you have LESS THAN
1 minute, 3 hours, or 18 months to live?

what if you BEAT the odds?

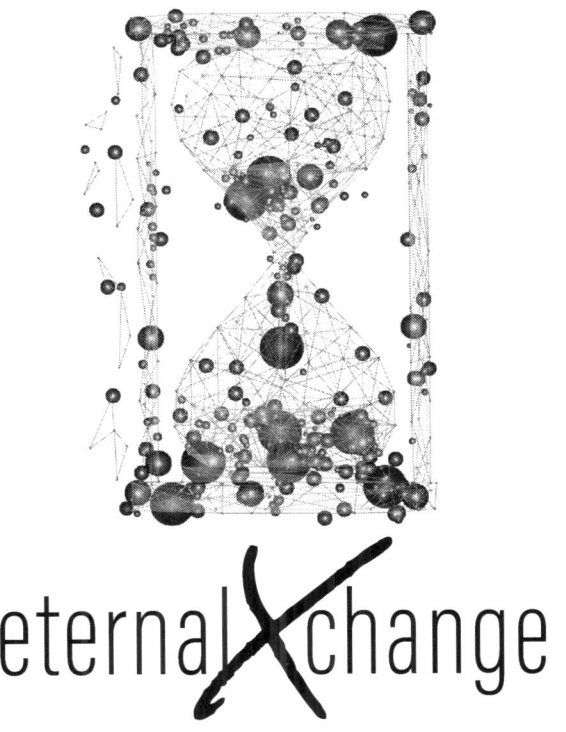

eternalXchange

legacy MOMENTS
Marilyn Seidl Sobwick

eternal✕change

Legacy Moments - Marilyn Seidl Sobwick

Self published by KPD Amazon, Seattle, Wa.

International Standard Book # 978-1-7347702-0-9

Printed in the United States of America

Contents

Three unlikely situations
lead to the unexpected!

The speedometer, a device we rely on
to make driving decisions, suddenly freezes
in place.

A growing tumor, born of mysterious origin,
poses deadly consequences.

Thirty feet below the ocean surface, where
depth pressure doubles, an over expanded
lung pops.

These moments in time were
documented for a couple reasons.

- to remind myself about
God's fervent message.

- to pass on to future generations
the grave importance of connecting frequently with our one and
only eternal advisor.

Preface

You're just doing life, minding your own business. Nothing seems to be out of the ordinary, until . . . your car slips out of your control, or you're diagnosed with a rare cancer, or your only chance to live is going under the knife of a stranger.

What's it like to beg for another chance to live, or to reach for every straw seeking answers for an unknown cure, or to receive unexpected help from the last place on Earth with your life at stake?

Who do you turn to when faced with grim circumstances? Are you prepared for the worst?

Hold on to your hat, because just doing life leads to the unexpected.

Flying Leap - 39 years old

Nearly hypnotized entrenched in thought, I'm in desperate search for answers concerning mounting marital matters when driving in heavy outer belt traffic. Green and white signs flash furiously before my eyes labeled by city names, highway numbers, and directional arrows. Letters and digits blend together in a field of green making it difficult to decipher a quick decision that demands a three lane changeover. I'm forced to snap to. "Get to the right!" shouts through my head. "Now! Get over now! Pressing the gas pedal, I peer over my right shoulder for oncoming traffic as the accelerator needle moves up rapidly: 55... 65... 70. Double checking my blind spot, the V-6 engine roars powerfully as I apply pedal pressure. Just then, a thunderous "Boom...Pound...Boom!" reverberates through my eardrums sending a shock wave of alarm through my body. My head whips back towards the windshield with my eyes locked directly on the speedometer needle frozen in place. The road in front of me is gone. I grip tightly with both hands on the steering wheel as if holding on for dear life. Shaking within, frantic fear sweeps across my face.

"What was that? Ice? Whoosh! What's happening?"

I'm stunned; I'm frozen in a moment of time.

Two hours earlier, I peek out my window, noticing huge cloud formations blending together like a soft-pillowed comforter: typical overcast weather for Ohio. I've planned a trip to West

Virginia to attend Marshall University's design conference only three hours away.

Glancing once again at this year's printed invite, it reads, "Influences," exploring graphic impressions artists have on society. In our fast-paced, go, go, get it, get it world, designers respond to meet clients ever-growing demands for market share. To be part of this invigorating program, I close up shop early to take part in the latest tricks of the trade. I'm packed and ready to go for the weekend.

Along the highway, I notice snow mounds piled high after being pushed against medians to keep lanes passable. During the night, freezing temperatures have turned them into heaps of frozen rock resembling life-size sculptures. Lined up like toy soldiers, they create roadside glacial barriers.

I'm preoccupied with pressing personal matters while heading toward an on-ramp to the Columbus outer-belt. My marriage, on the brink of collapse, casts uncertainty about how the days ahead will unfold? I reminisce. It's been fourteen years since our wedding day with my biological clock ticking. We haven't started a family, since Jim's only interest is getting ahead financially.

"Is financial gain the only goal in life?" Certainly not, in my way of thinking.

Beginning our journey together at age twenty-five, I marry an ambitious man who excels in athletics with an exceptional aptitude for business. Achieving his MBA, he sets out to make his millions in telecommunications. Two years into marriage, Jim encourages me to start my own graphic design studio, so,

I name it Logoz because my specialty is corporate identity marks. Characterized as DINKs, Double Income No Kids, we pursue our careers full speed ahead in power couple fashion. Fully engaged in Dublin community organizations, I hold a seat on the board in the Chamber of Commerce, the Arts Council, and the Women in Business. In the design community, my role is VP of CSCA, Columbus Society of Communicating Arts, and I'm an active member of D2G, Digital Designers Group.

"Could I be overly committed in community and business?"

Corporate America opens the door of opportunity for my husband's business prowess noticed by his superiors. Office women seek his attention for their own personal pursuits. He climbs the ladder of success with fiber-optic cable technology fueling his entrepreneurial enterprise. Mounting stress at the office leads Jim toward beer consumption now averaging 12-14 cans a night as his way of coping. My knight in shining armor embarks on his own path of destruction.

Back to the present, I'm in shock! With my hands clutched tightly to the steering wheel, a crowbar couldn't pull them off.

Lift-off erases all trace of traction as suspended, rotating wheels send a whispered murmur sailing past my ears. Then, a dead silence firmly surrounds me. Not a sound. I'm airborne. An eerie quiet makes time stand still. Insecurity slowly creeps into my being.

Feeling squeamish, my entire body draws back into the car seat in slow motion as I speed skyward. Inside, I'm pinned to my seat like the sensation of standing against a circular cage wall of the Round-Up amusement park ride. An invisible force presses against my chest, freezing me in place as if I'm being held hostage. Ferocious fear rushes through my entire body. I'm stupefied as I'm heading skyward.

Internal dialogue streams out of me. Silently, I'm screaming for God's help.

"What's happening? I'm scared. Is there a way out?"

I can't process this unfamiliar territory. Uneasiness weeps from every pore. Lost, forlorn, I'm driven to hopeless despair. Unwieldy, soaring, and out of control, I cling to the steering wheel, knowing full well I can't turn the car in any direction. Nor do I dare make any false move. Mounting anxiety stirs within me. Subconsciously, I know I'm way beyond the point of no return. It's curtains, my last act on earth.

Until now, I haven't come face-to-face with death. I confront my mortality. My fate's in God's hands. Instantly, I call out to Him. Ill prepared to leave life so unexpectedly, I'm fully engaged. Fatal thoughts spawn alarm.

"Will I be crippled? Will I become a vegetable? Please spare my family the agony of pulling the plug if I lie lifeless in a hospital bed. Am I going to heaven? Is this really happening?"

I'm reeling. Grasping aimlessly for any sign of reality, I turn my head to look around, only to notice milky white skies through my car windows. Nothing's in sight except a blank canvas without a point of reference.

"This can't be good. Is this heaven? Is this real time? Am I dreaming? If I shake my head, will I wake up?"

Physically shaken and mentally dumbfounded, rapid-fire snapshots of my life flash before me. Thrown into another level of consciousness, I sense I'm under a microscope of scrutiny. More questions pop into my head.

"Did I offer enough kindness to others? Did I help those in need?"

I might perish. There's nothing I can do. Nothing!

I'm instinctively drawn into a self-preservation cocoon. Realization sets in. I'm insignificant on God's examination table.

"God, am I no longer worthy? Is this my destiny? Is my number being called? Could I have another chance? Please forgive me for all my wrongdoings."

I beg for mercy. But, how foolish. Repentance and asking for forgiveness at this stage of the game is nonsense, considering this would be it!

With little time to sift through what might be considered a useless life, a stampede of nervous adrenaline rushes in. Amplified heartbeats pulse like drums, beating wildly from my chest. Anxiety races through me like raging fire. In utter disbelief, completely horrified, I plead earnestly.

"Can I get out of this alive? Will I be in heaven soon?"

As the car continues to soar skyward, Grandmother Seidl comes to mind. She recently passed away, and today, March 3rd, marks her birthday.

"Will I see her soon?"

In another flash of a second, a sensation of being light, like a feeling of weightlessness, overcomes me.

"What's this strange transition?"

A sharp, yet smooth, angle of rotation changes course in mid-air. It's airborne crest. Greeting gravity head on forces the hood down. My body rises, levitating me above my seat. Slanting towards the dashboard, my cross-shoulder harness catches diagonally across my chest, holding me in. Free-falling forward creates a vision of smashing through the windshield with broken glass piercing my body. Wrestling within myself, I'm emotionally conflicted.

Then, it goes from absolute quiet to an audibly thunderous ram. "Bam!"

Metal crunches, sending a signal of terror inside my space. I sense the car closing in on me. My right front tire forcefully slams the ground with a furious jolt, but bounces back up like a basketball on a polished, hardwood court. I continue to roll forward with a jounce, jerk, and ricochet.

Full-on impact triggers airbag detonation, sending an explosive gas bursting into my face, engulfing me in smoke. I gulp a quick sip of air, holding my breath to keep from inhaling the smelly cloud-like vapor.

Deployment instantly unleashes a violent attack on my body, tingeing my cheeks pink as if sandpaper has scraped them raw. At the same time, the sheer force delivers a fist punch, taking aim directly at my nose and ribs. Wedged between the safety air bag and seat back, I'm trapped.

Hammered down, my rear tires hit the ground aggressively, jolting the suspension system, rocking it back and forth like a seesaw as the car levels out on all fours. Instinctively, I slam on the brakes, holding steadfast with both feet on the pedal to stop forward motion.

Like a befuddled robot, I turn my head from left to right, observing that somehow I've landed in a lumpy field of grass.

"Is this heaven?"

Slowly, yet methodically, thoughts begin to re-assemble in my head. I've touched down on solid ground. It registers, I'm alive. I check my immediate surroundings, scanning side-to-side for potential danger.

Taking a short gasp, I puff out another breath. Miraculously, I've landed safely in a clearing to the right of the highway, away from traffic in either direction. I'm elated, ecstatic, but briefly. I turn my attention inside to check for broken ribs. Nothing protruding. Am I bleeding? No blood. A quick review determines that I'm still whole. I gasp an abbreviated sigh of relief thinking to myself,

"This airbag really works!"

Having just completed a pamphlet design for Ohio's Department of Motor Vehicles highway safety, the supplied photo depicts an airbag resembling a soft pillow of air. I just experienced otherwise. Instead, it's a stiff, rough canvas. Spared of being thrown into the windshield covered in shards of glass, the explosive impact leaves a sting on my face and soreness in my rib cage.

"Is my nose broken?"

The burning smell from lingering vapors is unsettling. I'm

not out of the woods yet. I blink to moisten my eyes. My throat feels a raw irritation, too. It must be from the cloud vapors still permeating. Staring into my rear view mirror, I'm frightfully aware that I could be in harm's way.

"Will the gas tank ignite?"

My former flight training suggests I need to move away from an engine crash. Immediately! Reaching underneath the airbag, I grasp the seat belt buckle, lifting for release. Click, click, it works! Wiggling in my seat while I'm still sandwiched between the airbag and my seat back, I lean forcefully, pushing against the door, while fumbling with my fingers for the inside latch. "Oomph! Oomph!" I'm still stuck shut. I let out a roar, tighten my shoulder muscle, push sideways and forcibly thrust my body into the door with a solid blow.

"Oh no, it's jammed! I've gotta get out of here!"

More fiercely determined, I slam against the door relentlessly, again and again. Beads of moisture gather on my brow. A nervously driven adrenaline rush in me rams the door with the power of a bull and,

"POP! Whew!"

The door gives way. I shimmy myself through the cracked opening just wide enough for me to squeeze out. Stepping away from the wreck a bit shaken, my legs take an unsteady stand beneath me.

With my chin tucked to my chest, each footstep penetrates the ground of an open field as if I'm walking for the first time. I rejoice inside with the realization that I'm standing on solid ground. Another motorist stops to approach me from across the highway.

"Are you all right?"

"I think so."

"Your car just flew above a semi."

"What?" I'm unable to fully comprehend. Then, the young man asks,

"What kind of car is this?" I reply, knowing it's the new car my husband let me borrow for this trip,

"An Acura."

"That was some kind of Evel Knievel stunt!"

Still in a daze about the incident, I feel a tremor of unsteadiness running through my body, seemingly an aftershock. I repeat silently to myself,

"I flew above a semi-truck. I flew above a semi-truck."

Across the highway, the driver points to a trucker who also stopped to call for assistance. Then, what seems to be only moments later, a helicopter circles overhead. The roar of rotary blades hover above me. Having landed in Columbus's metro area, a huge, red fire engine sounding its siren pulls up. Close behind, a medical service vehicle, beeping loudly with flashing lights, drives into the bumpy clearing with a team of quick responders surrounding me. I'm utterly amazed, stunned, at how "I" could alert so many emergency rescue crews. Shortly, a police car arrives with an officer walking towards me.

"Are you the driver of this car?"

I'm too intimidated to answer, but, in a soft voice, I clearly respond,

"Yes, . . . I am."

"Do you need any medical assistance?"

"No, I think I'm okay."

Then, the officer suggests,

"Why don't you sit down in the back seat of the cruiser while I fill out a report?"

Never having sat in the back seat of a cruiser before, this seemed like the safest place for me to be. Carefully, I answer the officer's questions, recalling what just happened. Thankfully, I sit erect on the front edge of the bench seat, knowing other drivers or vehicles weren't harmed in any way. In that moment, a feeling of warmth comes over me while giving heartfelt thanks to God for sparing others in my path.

With the report completed, we walk behind his cruiser to determine whether or not I'll need a tow truck. The police officer pries my car door open, noticing it's crunched, but he reaches in to stuff the deflated airbag back into the steering wheel compartment. He asks for my key to the ignition. The motor roars. When he taps the pedal, it begins to accelerate forward. Saving a tow truck expense, he asks,

"Can you drive your car behind mine?"

"Sure."

"I'll escort you back to the outer belt exit."

Sliding in behind the wheel of my "stunt" car, I limp down the road towards the off-ramp, waving goodbye to the officer as I park in Metro V's parking lot.

Although it's drivable for a short distance, I suspect from its appearance and rough sounding engine that it's probably totaled! How will I explain to Jim that I've wrecked his new car with his office only a few steps away?

Shutting off the ignition, resting the keys in my lap, I bow my head, closing my eyes in prayer. God's light shined on me. He spares me of what could have been a horribly tragic accident.

Miraculously, I land safely on the ground with only a few scratches and bruises, suggesting a divine intervention. Somehow, other drivers escape harm's way, too!

Ephesians 2:8
For it is by grace you have been saved,
through faith—and this not from yourselves,
it is the gift of God—

I can't help but think it's as if God's hand scooped me up in mid-flight and set me back down in a safe clearing. Within seconds, in a situation beyond my control, I'm in conversation with my higher power.

Our dialogue clearly depicts my humanness. In those few seconds, I'm reminded to develop a personal relationship with Him. With an instant replay of the accident, I lift my head, take a deep breath in, emit a sigh of relief, and utter my deepest heartfelt reply.

"Thank-you God. That was a close call."

After dropping by my husband's office to tell him about the

accident, he replies,

"What'd you do to my car?"

I'm stung with emotional pain. He's aloof. He cares nothing about my personal or emotional injury.

I reply.

"It's drivable!"

Fully aware of his sarcastic way, I flee from his less than sympathetic attitude by making a call to rent-a-car. Within the hour, the rental vehicle arrives. I transfer my bag, step in, and drive on to West Virginia.

On the road for three hours allows me time to sift through those terrifying moments. I feared for my life. I faced death.

Deuteronomy 4:29

But if from there you seek
the Lord your God, you will find him
if you seek him with all your heart
and with all your soul.

Surreal flashbacks swim through my head. I was helplessly caught up in a situation out of my control. When I was in the moment, I sat inside my soul. Up to this point in my life, I haven't been there, inside my soul facing death, that is.

"Is that what God wanted me to know?" That my soul needs tending to? It's overwhelming."

Reaching my destination by dusk, my design friends gather for dinner planned for us on campus. Quietly, I hold my story inside until the time seems right.

Slowly unraveling the tale about my drive to the conference, I share details about my Evel Knievel stunt and mid-air flight. Conversation ensues at the table, sparking their interest. Noticeable facial scratches, from the explosive airbag, confirms it's authenticity. Curious yet sympathetic ears give comfort, knowing they're my trusted comrades. Sharing my first-hand knowledge about rough, rugged airbags, I ask them,

"How do you know if you've got cracked ribs?"

I'm acutely aware of how it hurts to take in a deep breath. Catching abbreviated breaths makes it challenging to completely exhale. Achy and sore, I'm ready for bed feeling thankful I've been granted another day on earth. For now, it's enough to feel safe and blessed anticipating I'll be better by morning.

"Thank-you God. I don't know that I'll ever be able to thank you enough."

Held in the back of my mind, I lie awake, still recounting the incident. Slowly, nodding off from an emotional roller coaster, I close my eyes conferring with God,

"Yes, I need to sort it out."

He's got my attention!

afterthoughts

"If I weren't so deeply consumed with personal affairs could this accident have been avoided? Does being emotionally drained weaken my ability to effectively navigate life? And, to think, in a split second my mortality's in jeopardy! Is this a warning from heaven? Does this correlate to my crumbling marriage?"

It's clear, dreams of family and children are dashed with Jim's refusal of marriage/drug counseling. Without his willingness to participate as a couple, it's useless.

Jeremiah 6:16
This is what the Lord says:
Stand at the crossroads and look;
ask for the ancient paths,
ask where the good way is,
and walk in it,
and you will find rest for your souls.

Step, Skip, Run - 46 years old

Rolled into recovery, nine hours of anesthesia leaves me incoherent. An inkling of consciousness keeps me wandering aimlessly in a fog while weaning off drugs. I'm delirious. As if I'm in a recurring dream, I can't shake it off. Instead, I'm trapped in a continuous loop like in the movie *Groundhog Day*, where a TV weatherman finds himself reliving the same day over and over again. Plagued by utter restlessness, I'm on the edge of self-awareness, struggling deep within myself to find clarity. Intermittent shivers find a path to ripple through my body one quiver after another, after another. Those tremors trigger me into a few seconds of consciousness. Then, stronger, more intense vibrating waves shudder through my whole being.

"Make it stop," I scream within.

Gut-wrenching pain tears at me as if my insides are being devoured by vultures scavenging decayed prey. Deep within my midsection that feels like an open wound stabbed with stakes, fire-breathing dragons spew with rage. On a pain meter measuring 1 to 10, I'm way above 10. I can hardly bear it. Without warning, more involuntary convulsions ripple throughout my body uncontrollably. I cry inside,

"Stop, please stop, is anyone here?"

My eyelids open slightly, catching a glimpse of blurred images moving about in a dark, cavernous space. I manage to blink by loosening crusty discharge from the outer crevice of my eye.

"Am I waking up from a long night's sleep?"

Lying flat on my back, my spatial orientation is restricted! Drifting in and out of my surroundings, shadows of hospital staff scurry around me. As they mumble among themselves, I listen intently to decipher their dialogue, catching only sentence fragments to sort out.

"If only I could move my finger or toe, I'd get their attention."

Mentally focused, I strain to move my forefinger, then, my toe. But nothing.

"Am I paralyzed?"

Two months earlier, I'm lugging dive gear to shore, trudging up the sandy beach from the ocean's edge. My energy level drops dramatically, stemming from a queasy feeling coming from the pit of my stomach.

Everyone's expected to manage their own gear, including a heavy aluminum air tank, regulator, BC (buoyancy compensator), mask, fins, snorkel, and lead weights – standard equipment for most divers. I struggle to carry my apparatus to the outdoor spigot connected to a cement basin for rinsing, removing all saltwater.

A sluice of fresh water ensures my gear will last longer. Standing under an open air shower head, water streams over my full-body wet suit while I unzip and tug on the neoprene snuggly wrapped around my arms and legs to remove and hang on the line to dry. I'm feeling completely exhausted from routine scuba gear cleanup, barely reaching my thatched roof, single -room bungalow. Just short of the wooden steps, I stop to take slow, careful footsteps to the wooden deck.

A screen door closes behind me. Plopping backwards, I land in the middle of my cot, sinking deep into the mattress beneath a slow, rotating ceiling fan hanging down from the thatched roof. Nagging abdominal pain forces me to lie still to settle underlying discomfort brewing in my gut.

As the sun sets, my fellow Earthwatch divers celebrate local nightlife on the last evening of our Philippine expedition. In the distance, I hear playful, rhythmic beats of native drummers. What I wouldn't do to get off of this cot! I envision my comrades carefully balancing a drink in one hand while limbo dancing under a multitude of stars clearly visible in the moonlit sky. Physically immobile, I drown in my tears, missing out on an evening of native dance moves and local fare.

Warm, subtropical temps hang onto the night air, making it hard to fall asleep. Tonight, Balicasag Island holds still against even an occasional breeze. Moist glowing skin touching my sheets cools my internal temperature. I draw in a deep breath, pausing to exhale slowly to avoid more nausea.

Close by, a tree frog sings his mating call just outside my open-air window, croaking his harsh, hoarse utterance. Our tiny hut absorbs all creature sounds. By morning, frog tunes are replaced with a cock-a-doodle-do. Mr. rooster's internal clock goes off at the crack of dawn. No one sleeps in with him sounding off. But for now, I'm in dire need of rest. My eyes fixate on the hypnotic rhythm of the rotating ceiling fan blades. I lie still and finally doze off.

By morning, I've recharged enough to collect my dive gear, shorts and T-shirts, and I'm shoving them into my large, black canvas duffel. We hop aboard an open-air shuttle boat heading towards Manila, navigating the shallow turquoise island waterways. Perched on the edge of the wooden bench attached to the side of the boat, I breathe in the moist tropical breeze, feeling its warmth calm my nerves and unsettled stomach. Glistening waters replenish my desire to be part of this natural world in spite of feeling puny.

Leaving behind fourteen days of tropical paradise makes me sad, yet I'm grateful for my new friends of shared experiences. For lunch, we make a short stop on the island of Cebu, a larger, more densely populated island with amenities. A small gift shop sells brightly colored tropical fish T-shirts, perfect for souvenirs before we board our boat again heading North. Later, at the Ninoy Aquino, Manila's International airport (MNL), we say goodbye as fellow divers board planes to our respective destinations (i.e., England, Vietnam, Japan, and U.S.).

Once in flight, I'm relieved to be going home, leery about my physical stamina. Proud about our underwater research, monitoring ocean ecosystems, I peer through my tiny porthole, with our vast ocean beneath us. Thankfully, we're making noticeable progress, creating worldwide attention about the importance of sustainability.

back in the states

A few weeks later, during a routine massage, Angie, my masseuse says,

"There's heat radiating from your abdomen."

"Really? Oh . . . my stomach's been hurting since last month's dive expedition."

With her fingers, she gently traces the area.

"There's something here I haven't felt before."

"Should I have it checked out?"

"I would, and right away!"

From her tone of voice, I detected concern.

Three days later, an X-ray reveals a large mass residing in my abdomen. I can't see it, nor can I feel anything unusual under an area of normal abdominal tissue. But, detecting such a large foreign substance inside my gut caught my general practitioner's attention during my visit to his office. I didn't equate a queasy stomach with a squishy lump just below my belly button.

It's been over a month since my return from the Philippines, when I first felt stomach discomfort. Prior to the massage appointment, I sent stool samples to be tested for food poisoning at The Ohio State University's lab, turning up negative results. I'd even met with my gynecologist to rule out female problems. Nothing abnormal shows up until now. My GP's X-rays confirm all suspicions that something's physically wrong. This time, my doctor looks me straight in the eye and firmly suggests,

"Find a surgeon immediately. We'll make arrangements for a CT scan of your abdomen."

Phone calls set a plan in motion. A recommended surgeon, Dr. Schirmer, is in his early forties practicing at The Ohio State University Hospital. We meet, he reviews my films, and discusses the need for a biopsy prior to scheduling my surgical procedure. It all happens so quickly.

Flying in from Tulsa, mother knows I'll need aftercare assistance following the operation since I've been on my own for the past six years. I tell myself, living alone is better than being in a miserable marriage! As a girl scout, I've learned to be prepared, a trait instilled in me by my parents as well! While growing up, we lived in six different states including: Indiana, Massachusetts, Tennessee, Michigan, New Jersey and Ohio. It's as if we were early settlers in chuck wagons traveling to the next campsite. As we moved from place to place, we all prepared to greet every opportunity and address each new challenge. Today, I'm headed into another kind of challenge.

An early morning, thirty-minute drive from Dublin brings mom and me to the OSU Medical Center parking lot, where we gain access to the main entrance for further direction to the surgical prep station. Anxiously optimistic, I cheerfully engage in small talk as my way of letting the staff know I'm ready, entrusting confidence in their skill set. A pre-op nurse pricks my skin with a needle, prepping me for IV insertion. Briefly, I close my eyes, messaging God with a prayer to see me through. Fit and healthy at forty-six, my vitals are strong enough to tolerate this kind of invasive procedure.

Intently, I watch the anesthesiologist steadily pushing the syringe, injecting the drug meant to put me under. In walks Dr. Schirmer to confirm all parties are prepared to get underway. I, too, want to assure him I'm bravely confident about being a patient under his care. He places his hand on my shoulder when I begin to feel the drug quickly take affect. This is it! Figures fade into the background as my surroundings blur. I slide as planned into unconsciousness.

the procedure

According to my operative report, after the area is prepped, an incision is made vertically through my midsection. The surgeon pulls apart each side to gain access to my lower abdomen, where a six-centimeter, baseball-size tumor takes up residence. Building its home in my belly for at least the last three months, there it sits, the ticking time bomb! A pseudo capsule encases what appears to be a cancerous tumor.

Careful to avoid contamination to any other part of my body, it's skillfully excised. Any remnants left inside could be a source of recurrence. A remnant cell could trigger cancer re-growth. Like any toxic mass, all surrounding tissue, including organs, are removed to meet margins, the area surrounding the tumor.

Mother stands by, watching the hours pass before the waiting room door finally swings open with Dr. Schirmer approaching her. She stands up at attention, anxiously awaiting his report.

"The tumor's been removed." Mom breaths a sigh of relief.

"But, with your permission, we'd recommend a complete hysterectomy. I called in Dr. Bahnson, a specialist in urology, for a second opinion. By removing those organs, your daughter will have a better chance at recovery."

I'm currently childless. Mom knows a hysterectomy erases any chance of conceiving. And she, a breast cancer survivor, understands the devastating consequences of malignancy. After clearing a lump in her throat, she signs on the dotted line, giving full consent to proceed with the hysterectomy. Taking away her daughter's right to bear children wasn't anything she felt she'd ever be faced with.

Hospital pay phones only add to mom's frustration when she fumbles for change or recites her credit card number to the operator. Physically, emotionally and mentally drained mom finally reaches dad in Tulsa with a grim report. Meanwhile, my fate rests in the balance while supine on the operating table. Originally scheduled as outpatient surgery, I'm completely unaware of the complicated and time-consuming surgical procedure. Body parts are excised, labeled, and ready to travel on a one-way ticket to the lab, including the retro peritoneal mass (tumor), lymph nodes (gastrointestinal), uterus/tubes/ ovaries, colon, fallopian tubes, and some of my small intestine.

recovery room cont. - tremors

"Am I paralyzed?"

In the midst of unscrambling thoughts, battling for survival, my body shivers furiously until a dryer-heated blanket is snuggly tucked beneath me. Ah . . . a soothing calm ceases my incessant trembling.

Someone's attending to me. Oh, that feels so warm and comforting. But, all to quickly, the heat dissipates.

"Please keep those warm blankets coming!"

Hopeful anticipation becomes replaced with relentless torrents of ceaseless pain cutting through me like knives stabbing my abdomen. Going through my head is the "1812 Overture," where pounding explosive fireworks burst into the sky, like a big bang, a whizzing whistle, and thunderous thud as I lay strapped on a stretcher like Houdini in a straight jacket. I wince with each sharp pain. I plead to God.

"I don't know if I can hang on much longer. Am I dying?"

Incessant shaking with surge after surge of intolerable torment rumbles through me like a freight train until I can hardly stand it anymore.

"When will this end? Is this how Jesus felt when He suffered on the cross?"

A figure appears next to my gurney to collect my hand. I feel a faint sensation coming from the warmth of her gentle touch. LIFE. It's life! Does she instinctively know she's my only connection to a living, breathing existence? I greet her with a whisper sent from my dry motionless lips. Can she hear or understand my inner voice?

Psalms 39:7

And now, O Lord, for what do I wait?

My hope is in you.

"Please, don't let go," I plead.

I attempt to squeeze her hand, acknowledging her presence.

"I won't let go," she says.

Her life-healing power trails up my arm to my heart. Ah . . . I feel it. Is God sending his love through human touch? In that very moment, her kind, nurturing, patient-reassuring gesture plants a tiny seed of hope within me. HOPE. I rest in thought as my only reason to exist.

It's not long before a jerk of my gurney triggers my consciousness into a whirling, spinning existence. All of a sudden, an attendant steps in to whisk me away, releasing my hand from the nurse, my only connection to life.

"How could he?"

He steers me, rumbling and turning and rumbling again in and out of an elevator over the door tracks without careful consideration of my delicate condition.

"Easy, buddy."

He can't hear me because it's clear his only mission is to move my lifeless corpse from one place to another. And, he seems to be running a marathon with me in tow. Every bump and turn adds undue anxiety, agitating my frail state of existence.

Finally, I come to a brusque stop. Surprisingly, I didn't slide off. His shadow moves swiftly by my stretcher, leaving me all alone, stranded under brightly-blinding fluorescent lights.

"Hey, don't leave me here!"

He doesn't hear me, even if I could speak.

Uneasiness begins to consume me, turning my painful discomfort into perpetuating fear. Fear of being left all alone, helpless. Squinting beneath ultraviolet rays, I see nothing.

"Where am I?"

Fidgety, scared, physically hurting within, I eke out a muffled groan, pleading,

"Help . . . help!"

Pain pulsing from my gut persists, giving rise to me sounding off again,

"Help . . . help!"

Body shapes rush toward me like the cavalry. Familiar features slowly come into focus. Mom and my neighbor and dear friend, Lesa, advance to my rescue. Translating signals of anxiety through my eyes, Lesa calls for immediate assistance from hospital staff who, only when notified, check me in as a new patient.

"Is hospital personnel oblivious to me lying on a gurney in the middle of nowhere?"

After more deliberation, I hear staff discussing proper protocol about my arrival.

"Quit quibbling," I say to myself, "don't they understand I need attention?"

Mom and Lesa's startled stares trail up those tubes connecting my body to a variety of monitors like flexible arms resembling an octopus. I notice their faces flushed with shock, as they try to wipe away their astonished looks, trying not to frighten me. Dealing with my own distress cancels my train of thought. I struggle to communicate while staggering in pain. I'm vulnerably impatient.

"What's taking so . . . long?"

A nurse finally returns to administer pain meds. Within minutes, I feel, "Oh, that's better," a soothing sensation reclaiming a piece of normalcy within me. Finally, "ah . . .," relief at last! I'm neatly tucked under a sheet and feather-light, box-weave blanket, unable to offer conversation. My eyelids grow heavy with mom and Lesa slowly fading from sight at the foot of my bed. Comforted by the warmth of loved ones in my room, I let down my guard, nodding off. With their presence, I feel totally protected under their watch.

morning surprise

Startled by hospital personnel bustling through the door, Lesa jumps up from bunking on the stiff-cushioned couch. Lesa, a registered nurse, with a young family at home, relieves mom of her traumatic day by assuring her she'd keep a careful eye on me during the night and would call, should my situation change.

Lesa's experience with night-shift hospital personnel shortcomings and my extensive surgery urged her to stay with me through the first night. During a morning check, a young, less experienced nurse tries to adjust my endotracheal breathing tube, down my trachea, when suddenly, I can't breathe! My eyes grow wide as I clench my sheets tightly by my sides. Emotionally flushed, my heart starts to pound, as if outside my chest. Lesa calls for assistance. In the midst of commotion, she races to my bedside, advising the staff to gently guide the tube to its proper position. I inhale, gasping for air in the nick of time.

"Whew, that was a close call! What if Lesa hadn't been there? That could have been it!"

Awake after my first night's sleep, I'm coherent. Measured doses of fentanyl, administered intravenously, control my pain to tolerable levels. As my mind begins to clear, I'm finally able to unravel my thoughts. I'm told, I'm in The James.

"The James?"

Little did I know that after surgery, the hospital attendant rolled my gurney through a maze of underground passages between two different institutional entities; From The Ohio State University Medical Center to The James. Unconsciously, a page in my life turns overnight! Yesterday, I walked into the OSU Med Center for outpatient surgery. Ten hours later, I'm wheeled down corridors under a new facade, labeled, The James Cancer Research Hospital. Although no one says you've got cancer, putting two and two together removes all doubt. Tilting my head, bewildered, I never expected to be here, in "The James," that is! I ask internally,

"How long do I have to live?"

Within a day, my sister Carol flies in from Tulsa as part of the relief team. Mother needs family support even though my local friends assist her with directions on how to navigate Columbus. Carol walks in, briefed on my situation, but when she enters my room, her face is flushed, leaving her speechless. Blank stares cross between us, instantly translating her feelings of despair. Unable to hold my head up without being propped by a pillow, my interaction is minimal.

Growing up, Carol and I shared a room filled with childhood memories. Knowing one another well, we can gauge each others' emotions by simple facial expressions or body movements.

I'm thrilled to see her from my semi-reclined bed, yet, I perceive her sadness when she sees me. Her trip from Oklahoma to Ohio means my situation is serious, perhaps, even fatal! Yet, it warms my heart, seeing her while she offers mom reinforcement. With little to say, having tubes down my throat connected to apparatus, there isn't much for visitors to do but sit around thumbing through magazines or reading books while I doze off. I can tell Carol doesn't know how long I have to live. No one does! Doing my absolute best to show some physical improvement, I focus my attention on getting well. My only thought is, "recovery".

a visitor

Saundra's attention is drawn to my hospital bed, flanked by screen monitors, push-button apparatus, and IV stands, when she steps in. With a quick scan of the room, she pulls up a chair bedside like saddling a horse, with the understanding I'm unable to greet her as usual. We've been friends for some time, and over the years, we've become more like sisters.

Never expecting to find me laid up, she saw me as the one she would always rely on. In that scenario, I was between a friend and a mother to her. Where words of encouragement fall short, Saundra opens her bible and reads aloud. God's nourishing words offer direct access to my soul, which is now exceedingly vulnerable. I cling to passages as if it were the first time I actually heard them, since they now hold greater meaning. I ask myself in secret while listening to the sound of Saundra's peaceful and steadfast delivery,

"Am I prepared to enter the next place?"

"Clearly not, but hearing lines of scripture roll off her tongue touches my heart."

With the sound of another passage resonating within her voice, a tranquil stillness cradles me. Feeling soothed like a newborn being held by a mother, I sense my body levitating above the gurney in a bubble of warmth.

My eyes hold witness to an aura of soft light surrounding me. A physical transcendence of pure bliss completely envelopes my body, introducing me to a place of warmth and safety. I'm completely awe-stricken. An abrupt stop of scripture reading draws Saundra's gaze directed above my forehead, spawning an expression filled with glorious wonder. Mom, standing behind Saundra, looks up, too. In that moment inside, I'm wondering, "What is it? What would entice their surprised eyes with such undisputed countenance?"

Saundra closes her Bible and says goodbye for now.

first steps

Encouraging me to take my first steps by giving my left arm added support, mom offers assistance since it's the first time I've stood erect in days. Easing down from my elevated bed, I reach the floor, sliding into my hospital-issued slippers placed below my feet. Together, we do the baby-step shuffle, juggling an IV stand alongside a four-wheeled walker to steady myself.

Moving forward at a snail's pace, steps of caution remind me of Neil Armstrong's first step on the moon. Unlike Neil's giant step for all of mankind, independence from bed confinement denotes my major milestone. As we make our way out the room, just outside, behind my open door, a dark-skinned man with a wide push mop awaits patiently.

As witness to my first steps, he firmly stands intentionally in a darkened alcove with a calm demeanor and a reassuring smile. He speaks purposely, projecting his deep, resonating sound, offering mom a feeling of comfort by saying,

"She's doing fine and she'll be all . . . right."

Somehow, he knew. He knew mom needed to hear those very words at that moment! We press forward down the hall, then circle back to the room, but the gentleman with the mop is gone. Where did this wondrous sage of soulful voice go?

My private room is clean but sparsely appointed in this newly constructed, architecturally designed space filled with contemporary furniture. In the distance, I faintly hear elevators ring for access to my eighth floor accommodation.

The nurse station lies mid-hall, across from my room, situated within screaming distance, if necessary. On either side behind my bed is the latest in technological equipment to monitor my vitals. It's been a week before I have actually become acquainted with my whereabouts. Now that I'm able to walk and eat, the nurse tells me I can't go home until I pass gas. I say,

"What? . . . You're joking!" She explains,

"No, it's true, you run the risk of postoperative ileus if you don't pass gas."

Under my breath I say,

"Something as simple as passing gas keeps me hospitalized? Whew, our body's 'eco system!' "

Fortunately, in a day, my intestinal tract is up and running without any sign of blockage. It's now been seven days from admission to The James before I'm able to peer out my window, letting the sun's rays fall softly on my pastel-yellow summer dress, awaiting Dr. Schirmer's signature for release. I'm finally going home.

an angel

Weeks later after recovery from surgery, Saundra and I meet for lunch. During our conversation, I recall the peculiar moment during her visit at The James. I ask,

"Remember reading scripture in my hospital room?"

"Yes," she says.

"What did you see above my head?"

"I saw . . . , then she pauses, an angel!"

Her nonchalant tone didn't fluctuate or suggest anything out of the ordinary.

"What . . . an angel?"

Taken aback, I think she's kidding.

"Really?"

Her direct response didn't flirt with anything untruthful. She has no reason to lie about something like this. Especially since we've always spoken candidly about our beliefs, but, an angel? Seriously? Curious about this occurrence, I take it further.

"What did the angel look like?"

"She was smiling!"

It's not everyday an angel appears over one's head. Then, I remember the blissful aura of comfort surrounding me like some sort of spiritual sensation, perhaps transformation, when lying in my hospital bed. Was I feeling the presence of heaven?

Our exchange moves me, and I instantly accept this spiritual visualization as fact. There must be reasons why phenomena happens. Soul-stirring thoughts of my past make me wonder if I've been living randomly, without direction. Somehow, this "angel" incident gives life clear meaning, a reason to be. Should I follow subtle clues, cues, intuition and encounters to guide me? Elated about the angel smiling, I beg for more,

"What else? What was she wearing?"

"A smile, the angel was wearing a smile!"

My heart instantly believes. As eager as I am to know details, somehow I understand these words complete her vision. A grateful sigh of contentment fills me. It makes perfect sense. The feeling of calm coming over me in my hospital bed came directly from heaven. Perhaps the angel's smile meant I was safe from harm under God's protection. Saundra finishes by saying,

"I believe you're cured!"

Driving home from lunch, it occurs to me that perhaps the man holding the mop just outside my room door was meant to be there, too! Perhaps he was a messenger from heaven. What compelled him to speak to us with his reassuring look and stately stance, resembling a figure of highest authority? Visually, he reminded me of the "American Gothic" portrait, where the farmer stands next to his pitchfork. Was he an angel? My guardian angel? He was there for a moment and then gone. Yet, so . . . real!

oncologist follow-up

A month passes before I meet with a local oncologist appointed to my case. My drive there is only ten minutes with a short wait before I'm ushered into a room to take my vitals. Dr. Stanek enters the room, introduces himself, then leans back against a white cabinet while holding a manila folder open directly in front of him.

I'm especially cheerful since surgery's behind me. And besides that, I'm feeling physically stronger every day. Perched on the examining table with my legs criss-crossed at my ankles, I'm anxious to hear his follow-up report. Listening intently, I tilt my head to reach his gaze, fixated everywhere but in my direction. While his eyes search for corners of the room, he utters,

"I hate to be the one to tell you this, but according to the post-op results, a rare and deadly cancer called a leiomyosarcoma was excised."

I didn't have a reply, but under my breath, I said,

"That means nothing to me since I've never heard of a ly-o-my-o, dot, dot, dot. And, what about congratulations for my excellent recovery? Plus, I'm certain I heard the words 'spindle cell' uttered while I was in the recovery room."

Since he didn't hear a word of that, he goes on to say,

"Follow-up treatments, such as chemotherapy and radiation won't have any effect against this kind of cancer."

"What?" I say aloud.

I question myself in silence again,

"Why is he talking like I still have cancer? The tumor's been removed. I'm healing."

Still sitting at attention on the examination table, I try to sift through what sounds like mumbo jumbo. I get the feeling I'm being punished. Shattered by his words, I'm totally speechless. Then, out of nowhere, he comments,

"My nephew died from a leiomyosarcoma a few years ago. He was only twenty-three years old, an athlete and in perfect health."

"I'm very sorry to hear that."

He goes on to say,

"The problem with this soft muscle cancer is that there aren't any significant symptoms until it's too late. And, because it grows rapidly, metastasis is probable."

I sigh. Lucky for me, my masseuse found my tumor. I'm healing. But then, his last three words echo as if I was standing in the Grand Canyon, "*metastasis is probable!*" It finally hits me. My stomach starts to churn. I'm in total disbelief.

"Metastasis?" I mumble within.

He adds,

"Here's what I can do for you. I'll call my colleague at Cleveland Clinic to get a second opinion."

While sorting out his words, he leads me to a brown leather couch in a casual sitting area outside his private office. My world goes into slow motion as I ease into the soft leather, tufted cushion, placing my left elbow on the armrest. Still dumbfounded, I lean further left to peer through his office door. His backside is reclined in the comfort of his easy chair as he makes the call. My mind races to make sense of his shocking diagnosis. Ten minutes later, he steps out.

"My colleague concurs. You now have two professional opinions! All you can do is wait to see if your cancer shows up again."

Wham! His diagnosis hits me like a baseball bat. Not only am I not out of the woods, but I'm being forced to subscribe to an ongoing battle with cancer. This is simply unacceptable. How can a surgically removed tumor still pose danger? Metastasis without a path for prevention doesn't fit into my plan of recovery.

Keeping this all to myself, I stand up, shake his hand, and say goodbye.

Physically, I freeze in place for a moment. As if in a trance, I pull my purse up to my shoulder, stare blankly into space and struggle to place one foot in front of the other. A daytime sleepwalk takes me outside into the parking lot, where I turn around a few times, looking for my car. Reduced to hopelessness, my legs start to go weak. Where's the car?

On the brink of collapse, I frantically search my purse, fumbling to find my key fob. I press the fob and click, I hear it unlock. The sound directs me to run and hop inside my car, securing my place of safety. I fall into the seat and sit in silence, not knowing whether to scream or cry. My eyes well up. I cup my hand to sweep away a tear rolling down my cheek. With a deep breath, I close my eyes. My head drops forward.

"Okay, God, now what? Do I get my affairs in order? Or, is this an endurance test of faith?"

That night, I toss and turn in bed, wrestling with uncertainty. I couldn't give into the idea of metastasis, at least not without a fight. And, up until now, I've been in the process of regaining my strength. I'm not about to give up on that momentum.

Why should I let those doctors determine my fate? After a

long, restless night, I wake up with the idea that it's time to regroup, sift through my options, and create a plan of action. I didn't waste time researching to set up appointments with medical doctors who specialize in diagnosis and treatment of cancer. Since the Ohio oncologists left me hanging, I'm more determined than ever to move forward in search of second, third and fourth opinions, if necessary.

1 Peter 5:7
Cast all your anxiety on him
because he cares for you.

Mayo Clinic

One of the first institutions to come to mind is the world-renowned Mayo clinic in Minnesota. For patients like myself, ailing from unusual or unknown diseases, Mayo, with its worldwide reputation as a leader in medical technology, is my next option. A few phone calls set my plan of action into motion.

With the date set, I call my older sister Pat, who's an RN, to ask if she's able to accompany me. With her full-time position as the head of Human Resources for Blue Circle Cement, she manages time off to travel from Albany, NY, to meet me. With a few weeks' notice, the day has finally come when we board our flights from different cities to rendezvous within an hour of each other to Rochester, Minnesota.

After I'm settled in my seat, I hear the engine start up. Peering through the porthole following airport directionals, I notice we're heading onto 28L from the taxiway for take off. For me, it's automatic to check runway headings.

In my early 30s, I picked up my pilot's license through The Ohio State University's flight school. Flying with dad, who was also a private pilot, gave me the bug. Training started in a 152 fixed-gear, two-seated Cessna, is barely big enough to accommodate two adults. For me, at five-feet-three, it was the right size. Then, I progressed to fly 162s, 172s, and 182s, needing a seat cushion to see out the front windshield.

"Oh, the exhilarating feeling of soaring the skies on a sun-filled day, leaving earth and its problems below."

During flight training, we'd roam the Ohio countryside, executing power-off landings and making radio contact with the control tower for permission to take off and touch down. Laughter always filled the de-briefing rooms with student pilot mishaps. One of my fellow pilots continually got lost during her solo flights. Thankfully, I've always had a keen sense of direction.

After lifting off the runway to meet my sister, the plane makes a turn in an unexpected direction. Are we being hijacked? I'm not panicked, but the thought crosses my mind. I know we should be going north to Minnesota, but instead we're heading east. How can this be happening? My arm reaches above my head, pressing my finger on the call button for the flight attendant. I ask,

"Where is this flight headed?" She replies,

"We're going to Rochester, New York."

"Rochester, New York? My ticket says Rochester, but my intention is to go to Rochester, Minnesota."

"You're not the first to have this mix-up. Once we land, just go to the ticket counter and reschedule."

"Oh, I will!"

"Not to worry," I say under my breath as I begin to stir within, not that she'd fret. Since my clinic appointment is scheduled for early morning, I run to the US Air counter when we land. Stepping up to the agent, I wait til I have her attention before asking,

"When is the next flight to Rochester, Minnesota? I'm supposed to be in Minnesota, not New York!"

Her lips crease wide across her face with a casual expression of knowing.

"This is a very common mistake between our two cities. Sadly, it happens all the time."

Since I'm not in the mood to exchange pleasantries, desperate to reach my destination today, I blurt out,

"I'll need a flight to Minnesota."

She starts punching in keys on her keyboard and views the screen of schedules and replies,

"I'm not seeing any flights going there until tomorrow."

"Tomorrow? I've got to get there tonight!"

Then, I'm quick to ask,

"What about going through a second city, like Cleveland or Detroit?"

She punches more keys.

"Let me see."

I sigh, nervously awaiting. I think to myself, "How could this have happened? Have I lost my mind, too? Is this 'cancer thing' affecting my brain as well? I notice the agent nodding.

"Okay, I can get you on a flight to Detroit connecting to Rochester. It won't get in until 10:31 p.m. this evening."

"I'll take it."

"It'll leave from gate A-9 in two hours."

I wait for her to hand me a new ticket to my intended destination and quickly call Pat from my cell.

"Hello, Pat. You're not going to believe this, but I'm in Rochester, New York!"

"You're kidding!"

"I wish I were."

I squirm inside myself, thinking about the flight mishap that could've ruined the entire plan. Rescheduling my Mayo clinic appointment was out of the question, plus, I wasn't about to pay for two more round-trip flights and another hotel stay. And, besides that, Pat has used the remainder of her vacation days to assist me with this medical advice.

"It's a long story, but I should arrive at the hotel between 11:00 and 11:30 p.m."

I detect Pat's disappointment from the tone of her voice, but she knows I'll get there, despite missing our afternoon together. Picking back up with an optimistic pitch, she keeps me encouraged by saying,

"I'll be here!" Oh . . the sound of her optimism felt good.

Mayo bound

A brisk morning walk from our hotel to the clinic's main campus allows an on-time arrival for my 8 a.m. appointment. As we turn the corner, I gasp at the sight of Mayo's massive, impressive front entrance facade. Straight ahead, we clearly read in silver metallic letters, Mayo Clinic, in all caps.

"Is this my new ray of hope hidden behind this impressive entry?"

Pausing in front of the automated front doors, I stop short, tapping Pat's shoulder.

"Thank you for being here with me."

"I'm very glad to be with you." She smiles assuredly, wrapping her hand around my forearm.

Medical jargon fills the halls as we walk into this grand establishment where 3,700 physicians, scientists and researchers collaborate. A league of medical experts will review my case and offer their opinion about my prognosis. Swirling through my head is the notion that this is the world's best medical facility to seek treatment. I'm prepared with medical records plus a private family nurse. Pat could speak their language, ask direct questions, and help me decipher their medical vernacular.

Droves of people suffering with illnesses fill the chairs in the expansive waiting areas. It looks as if we're all being processed for immigration. Hearing my number called, I'm pricked in a open-air station to provide blood samples, followed by an arm wrap to check my blood pressure along with my pulse taken. It's like some sort of an assembly line. This isn't the nurturing one-on-one, top notch care facility I'd envisioned.

The two of us are finally directed into a typical patient room while the Mayo Clinic dream team reviews blood and urine samples, as well as the medical documents I brought with me. A threesome in identical white lab coats enter the room, shaking our hands while introducing themselves. One speaks up on behalf of the team,

"We've all reviewed your paperwork together and have collectively come to a conclusion. This is a rare type of cancer with just a few case studies. There's really nothing you can do unless it returns. We suggest you wait and see what happens! Any questions?"

We're in shock and have nothing to ask. Following his brief oral summary, they look at one another, nod in agreement, close their folders, turn about-face, and file out the door, one behind the other. I draw within myself asking,

"What? No hope? No plan of attack?"

Pat and I look at one another in astonishment. In our body language exchange, Pat raises her eyebrows and I shrug my shoulders. With high expectations from such a well-respected institution, I'm stung in a moment of disbelief.

"That's it?"

Pat's as surprised as I am. How could this internationally highly recognized health institution treat a patient so coldly with their desensitized, robot report? Even though it may be on par with Columbus and Cleveland Clinic oncologists, don't they have a higher polished level of patient interaction and personal care solutions? With such a grim reality to face, we walk out like zombies in just enough time to board our planes. All I could think about during the flight home is, what a waste of time and money for both of us. I'm emotionally drained.

one more opinion

Being true to myself, I can't let Mayo's opinion be the last word. So, I press on by going to Columbia University Hospital's Medical Center in New York. The Big Apple is where I meet the foremost expert concerning leiomyosarcoma research.

From Newark's airport arrival gate, I step into a New York city taxi, traveling north through Lincoln Tunnel to reach the unforgettable sights and sounds of this amazing metropolis. My heart races with fond memories of special times spent here with family and friends.

On more than one occasion, I saw the Rockettes at Radio City Music Hall, followed by dinner at Mama Leone's. Another time, I took in Broadway performances like *"Phantom of the Opera"* and *"1776."* Numerous visits to museums like the Met (Metropolitan), Guggenheim, and MOMA (the Museum of Modern Art) filled my head with life's wondrous works by well-known, talented artists.

"Am I coming to the end of those fun, enriching cultural experiences?"

Arriving at Columbia's Med Center, I enter the lobby and read a wall plaque directing me to Dr. Taub's floor. During my elevator ride, I anticipate fresh insight about my health status from yet another oncology specialist. Down the hall and through a couple of doors, I face a tall, distinguished doctor wearing his white lab coat, who looks to be in his mid-sixties. After introductions and casual small talk, he reviews my CT scans and surgical and lab reports I've brought while I await in anxious anticipation. Since I'm here by myself this time, I ask,

"Would you mind if I record our conversation?"

He replies, "That's absolutely fine," having been asked this question more than once before.

I pull out my pocket-size recorder and lay it on the table. His bedside manner is welcoming with his calm, sincere demeanor resembling that of my own father. He begins by saying,

"According to my case studies, the odds from your type of cancer are better than breast cancer, in that, if this cancer doesn't return in three years, it's never coming back!"

My ears perk up. What? Did he just say something positive? This sounds like a ray of hope. The thought of recovery resonates in my mind, even if just for a moment. He goes on to say,

"Should this cancer return, I want you to come to New York for surgery. We have a very experienced team here."

Unlike my previous appointments, this caregiver didn't send me away to fend for myself. Even if his diagnosis aligns with the Ohio and Minnesota oncologists, he caps the "watch and wait" period at three years. The status of my deadly cancer did not change, but like a guardian, he makes sure I understand he'll provide care for the duration, however long it may be. He continues,

"I've had a few of my patients try an experimental drug called thalidomide, . . . you may have heard of it."

"Gee, . . . that sounds familiar."

"It was used during the 1950s for women with morning sickness. But, the drug was outlawed when infants were born without limbs. Today, it's been re-introduced to starve off cancer cells in the body, so we've offered thalidomide to our patients. There's no guarantee this will work, but the only side effect reported from this drug is sleepiness, resulting in minimal risk. Your other option is to do nothing and wait it out."

I contemplate and reply,

"I've got nothing to lose by taking thalidomide?" With a 90% chance of cancer recurrence within 18 months, I'll reach for any medical breakthrough or sign up for any trial drug test. As part of a clinical study, I could even help research.

"Yes . . . I'll try it."

Dr. Taub acknowledges my request by saying,

"I'll make contact with the drug supplier and your medical insurance company. The prescription can be sent directly to you."

"Great."

With enough time to make my pre-scheduled flight back to Ohio, I wave for a taxi back to Newark.

Proverbs 18:10
The name of the Lord is a strong tower;
the righteous run into it and are safe.

creating a plan

Exhausted from a day of travel, I fall asleep easily when back in Ohio. The next morning, I sprawl out supine on my king bed, agonizing because absolutely no one in this world has enough medical knowledge to cure me.

Feeling sorry for myself won't lead anywhere, either. My eyes close. I think about heaven. Reaching deep within myself, the notion occurs to me,

"Hey, there are cases when God still cures people, right? Yes! God's it! Only God can cure me!"

If He decides to cure me, His plan is foolproof! Up till now, human remedies lack certainty. In prayer, I thank God for subsiding my physical pain. At this moment, I know He has a plan for my unforeseeable future, but I don't because, well, I'm human.

Psalms 46:1

God is our refuge and strength,
an ever-present help in trouble.

Each new day, I pray for my "energy" to return. With God as my cure, I collect my thoughts by reading the Bible, joining Bible study groups, and routinely attending church service /Sunday school classes. After all, that's the least I can do to honor Him.

It goes without saying, I'll volunteer my design talents for all printed works the church may need, indefinitely. Of course, God doesn't need my help, but He does require my faith to follow His heavenly plan.

In the meantime, my earthly plan includes researching the web by reading articles preventing cancer by investigating alternative methods to cope with my circumstance. While some inflicted patients create imaginary battlefields in their minds of mini-pac men eating cancer cells, my plan depicts a baseball field scenario, including 1st, 2nd, 3rd and home. Coming from a need to be creative, I entitle it, "*Covering my Bases.*"

Hebrews 11:1
*Now faith is being sure
of what we hope for and certain
of what we do not see.*

Covering my Bases
Baseball Field Scenario

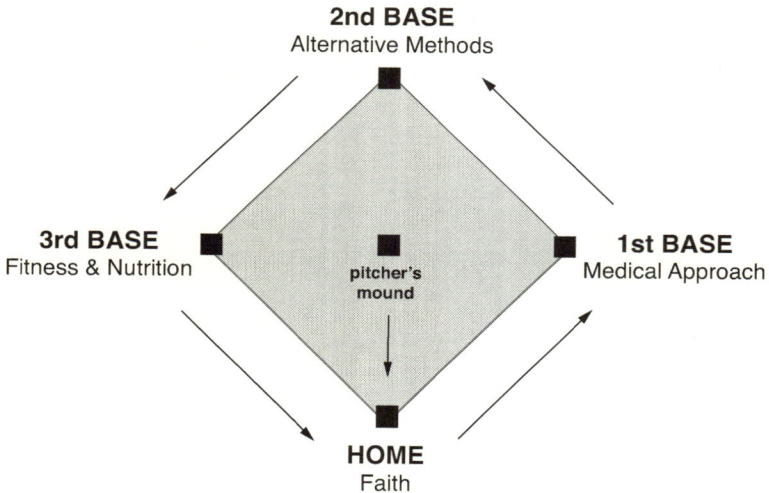

2nd BASE
Alternative Methods

3rd BASE
Fitness & Nutrition

pitcher's mound

1st BASE
Medical Approach

HOME
Faith

From the pitcher's mound a hard ball comes straight at me, so, I take off to 1st base in search of a medical cure. Without success, I hop to 2nd base to explore alternative methods. Skipping to 3rd base, I turn to fitness and nutrition for my own health and well being. In the process, the pitcher keeps throwing a ball to home plate where I run to discover my ultimate cure is faith in God. *A HOME RUN!*

1st base - medical approach

My first plan of action starts with thalidomide, the experimental drug prescribed to wage battle against my leiomyosarcoma prescribed by Dr. Taub. Determined that this formulated compound will starve off any invasive cancer cells, I begin the program in October, increasing the dose gradually.

family gathering

Starting the thalidomide regime happens to coincide with an impromptu family gathering in Oklahoma. Dad's 80th birthday is next May, but now, considering my circumstance, my sisters step up the reunion, choosing this coming November to honor his milestone. Intuitively aware of my unpredictable future, I'm given the opportunity to see everyone again, perhaps for the last time. Not to sound morbid, but I'd be lying if I didn't say it crossed my mind.

Mutual understanding pulls us together, especially when a crisis arrives, which is something dad instilled in us since we were very young. That is, we collaborate as a family to resolve issues. This stems from the idea that two heads are better than one. So, this year, unlike any other year, just before Thanksgiving, we gather in a secluded, picturesque, rustic hunting lodge perched high on a rocky plateau, not far from Tulsa. We've arranged to have the entire facility to ourselves for this very important family gathering.

Authentic hand-built details grace this thoughtfully designed stone-covered, three-level structure, featuring a warm, welcoming entry. Bavarian-style wood railings accentuate a spacious porch surround, giving us access to sunset views of expansive prairie lands across the plains.

Charming mahogany French doors open into a huge great room with a wood-burning stone fireplace and uniquely handcrafted, fully stocked bar. Round leather bar stools turn a full 360° where our youngest members take turns spinning each other around. Sinking into deep-seated brown leather couches, we settle into our surroundings, fully entertained, greeting everyone beneath a quaint, architecturally lofted room.

Adjacent to the main area, an opening leads to a cozy beamed-ceiling dining nook where a delicious catered dinner awaits us, dare I say, a "last supper," with our extended family of fifteen. On a side table, flown in from an Ohio bakery, sits a specialty design birthday cake, made to look like a present with a gold bow made of fondant. Spread between layers of moist cake is raspberry filling to sweetly satisfy the finish of our feast.

My brother-in-law hangs a banner entitled "Big O's 80th Birthday Bash" to set the tone for our reunion, roasting dad, AKA grandpa, to the younger family members. We all gather underneath the sign to pose for the camera, preserving the memory.

Moving to a lower level club room where hunting gear is stored, a projector runs a slide show of family portraits that reveal lifetime stories and pokes fun at embarrassing moments.

No one is spared when it comes to roasting one another. As family photographer, I've collected and created duplicate photo albums holding treasured photos to share memories of our times together. Healing laughter fills the room, overpowering those hidden fears about what tomorrow may bring.

We disband to the grand room where a pool table entices billiard competitions. Others are shuffling cards for a friendly game of hearts and the sound of tiles clatter when scattered on another table for dominoes. Before retiring, we gather on comfy leather couches for a spontaneous game of charades, and good 'ole togetherness chats.

Up the wooden staircase, bedroom suites feature plush white towels and bathrobes neatly folded at the foot of each bed. Happily accommodated under one roof in our prairie setting, my family celebrates our love and respect for one another under the stars in the land where buffalo still roam. I feel God's loving arms surround us on this evening of treasured memories.

Able to keep up with the group for awhile, I begin to feel side effects of thalidomide the next morning as I struggle to wake up, arriving late for a huge country breakfast. Family already gathered around the wooden table would soon pack to go home, making every moment remaining more precious. This reunion, a gift of love in our picturesque setting, sends us on our way, never to be forgotten.

intuition

Shaking off an overwhelming daze becomes challenging, especially in the weeks ahead. As thalidomide dosage increases, I begin to resemble a walking zombie, feeling sluggish throughout the day, a side effect Dr. Taub spoke of. At times, my head's in a fog. On a morning jog, I feel an unusual, tingling sensation in my fingertips and toes. This slight prickling brings to mind the effects a fetus might have experienced when born without limbs, giving them the label, thalidomide babies. I confront myself right then and there. This has to stop. Constant drowsiness is not at all like the person I knew myself to be. In December, I make the decision to quit taking thalidomide. My conversation with God concludes,

"Whatever time I have left, I need to be my authentic self, with a clear mind and a pure heart. My genetic DNA supports nothing less."

Placing myself in God's hands with prayerful exchange, I take one more step toward putting my faith in Him. I recite to myself,

"What will be, will be."

CT scans

Prescribed by my New York oncologist, I undergo periodic CT's, computerized tomography. A regimen starting with a scan every month for three months followed by a scan every other month for six months, then, one every three months to take me through 18 months. This imaging provides a recorded map of my interior, keeping a close eye on any changes that may arise.

Preparation for a CT requires picking up formula from the drug store, a coconut milky liquid, AKA, contrast, to drink prior to scanning. When in the gastrointestinal tract, the radiologist can see the area highlighted. With a thirty-five minute drive to reach the facility, I swallow the remainder of the awful, thick, milky stuff, barium-sulfate, in the parking lot before entering the building. Yuk! I ask myself,

"Why can't medical formula scientists consult culinary taste kitchens before test marketing patients? As bad as this tastes, anything would be an improvement."

The thought of downing another bottle of barium-sulfate makes me sick to my stomach.

Patients in the waiting room wear athletic attire with elastic waistbands acceptable for scanning. Patients disguised as athletes make me smirk. Zippers, belt buckles or anything metal can't be worn during X-rays. Shallow stares cross the room in silence as each of us in athletic wear wait to be called in next.

I'm led through a hall to a room where a huge doughnut-shaped machine sits and a horizontal platform protrudes from its center. After removing my shoes, following the radiologist's instructions, I lie face up. An IV is inserted in my forearm when the attendant finds a visible vein. Then, an iodine-based substance sends a heat sensation trailing up my arm, leaving a metallic taste in my mouth. The flavor isn't objectionable, just foreign-tasting. Unlike the barium-sulfate, this solution enhances a view of internal organs and soft tissues, like muscles, arteries and veins: another marker for the radiologist. As I lie quietly, the tech pushes the button, allowing the flat bed to move my outstretched body slowly into the doughnut tube hole up to the chest area. Click, click, I hear a humming of the cylindrical machine start up. Then, another sound like a ball being rolled onto a roulette wheel circles about. Then, a tic, tic, tic noise, as if the winning ball has dropped into a slot. The ticking stops. I'm told my internal parts are being photographed in slices.

Lights flash on the panel above my head. A blink of color tells me when to hold my breath for at least 20 seconds. A slow exhale allows clearly precise, photographic captures of cross-sections. Once again, like every appointment, I close my eyes and pray deeply that nothing harmful is detected. Asking God to calm my fears, dwelling on the positive, I'm fully aware that my results could go either way. I prefer to concentrate on trusting Him since I know it's not up to me.

Nahum 1:7

The Lord is good, a stronghold
in the day of trouble;
he knows those who take refuge in him.

2nd base - alternative methods

My sister Carol stays connected with other colleagues in psychology, attending conferences now and then. Surfing the net, she pulls up information on a speaker from a recent conference in Arizona. The conference talk covered the concept, "Alternative Methods of Spiritual Renewal," through a process called "getting centered." This topic triggers Carol's call to me.

"Hey Marilyn, I just thought about the speaker from my last conference in Phoenix. Her discussion on alternative methods of spiritual renewal might be helpful to you."

"Oh..., I'm listening"

"The method is entitled, *Getting Centered.*"

Does Carol think I've lost my mind?

"*Getting Centered,* really?"

Carol explains further.

"It's more like a support program."

"Oh, okay."

Poring over my thoughts about being on a "*wait and see*" program without a cure, this option sounds like something I could do in the meantime.

"Gee . . , I'd like to do what I can!"

A support program might be a good idea since I've got nothing to lose and, perhaps, something to gain.

Carol replies,

"Maria is traveling to Ohio next month to offer private

sessions. Would you like to schedule an appointment with her?"

Carol describes Maria as an "elder," someone sought after and entrusted for counsel because of her experience in this field.

"Sure, maybe. Send me the info and I'll check it out."

With Carol's persuasion, or should I say, gentle nudge, I make plans to meet the Arizona speaker, Maria, in Ohio.

harmony farm

Within a two hour drive from home, I find myself in a scenic but remote nature preserve near Dayton, Ohio. A sign reads, *Welcome to Harmony Farm, a Wellness Studio.* I see a path near the parking lot leading me to a beautiful outdoor pool with a huge waterfall, sending tranquil, trickling water down the rock wall to the water below. Next to the pool is a spa where guests schedule a massage or where one can receive energy work along with wellness coaching and mindfulness, AKA meditation. Now, I understand why the slogan on the website says, *"release your mind, relax your body, and restore your heart."* The scene is one of serenity and peace. Behind a glass-walled structure, I approach a lady behind a desk where I notify her of my scheduled meeting.

Since my appointment is with the visiting elder, Maria, I'm ushered in to be introduced. She's a middle-aged, healthy- weight woman with olive skin who carries features characteristic of Mexican descent. Outfitted in comfortable clothing, Maria has an unassuming appearance, even though she's a professional psychologist. The two of us are led to a cozy room lit by natural light peeking in from a small window. As the door closes behind us, Maria points to a chair, inviting me to share my recent health history. Comfortably seated, but not knowing where to start, I begin with the present,

"My cancerous tumor's been removed, but now, I face possible recurrence. I've learned cancer is a tricky disease. Case studies show that even if a tumor's removed in one part of the body, cancer remnants migrate elsewhere and plant new roots." I go on,

"According to several oncologists, I have a 90% chance my cancer will return within 18 months."

Maria replies, nodding with full understanding by sharing her experience in a calm, soothing tone.

"I, too, have had cancer. Healers helped me. Now that I've been cured, I've dedicated my life's work to assist others. This process calls upon God to send his healing energy."

"Okay . . . "

My tone of voice lowers, sounding a bit leery. Resting in thought, I ask myself,

"Who said anything about healers?"

Feeling apprehensive, I try not to squirm, reconsidering. I guess healers can be a support group, in a sense. I recall faith healers seen on television where followers faint, right on the spot, by the touch of a hand. I've never witnessed this in person, but I can't help but wonder if those accounts were staged for a camera, or, if the inflicted really received healing power.

Feeling some trepidation about this new approach, I remind myself, this was all Carol's idea. I respect her professional recommendation and guidance, so I sit still and listen. Maria motions with her hands and says,

"To start, . . . lie face up on the floor."

Lying down makes me even more vulnerable, but I remind myself,

"I paid BIG bucks for this so-called treatment."

Maria closes the shade to darken the room, kneeling slowly to the floor by my side.

With a soft voice, she says,

"Close your eyes and concentrate on taking in deep breaths. Then, exhale slowly."

She places her palms flat down, conforming to the curvature of my forearm. This technique, I remember, seems to be commonly referred to as *laying on of hands*. She bows her head and begins to commence conversation with God, imparting spiritual blessings upon me. She whispers loud enough for me to hear her request, inviting God's presence. She continues by saying,

"Slow your breathing. God's healing light energy will shine on me. His energy will travel through me, then into you."

After a pause, she whispers,

"Inhale with your nose and exhale through your mouth."

With inflection in her voice, she slowly repeats,

"In with the GOOD, out with the BAD."

Following direction, I do my best as a willing participant in this unusual exercise. A flow of rhythmic breathing creates sound waves, filling the small room. I repeat this process over and over and over again.

"Breathe in the GOOD, breathe out the BAD," she repeats.

Silently, I think to myself,

"And this will help? I'll hyperventilate!"

Doing my best to continue the rhythm and flow, I allow myself to relax. Several minutes seem like hours, considering my only role is to breathe slowly. After awhile, Maria closes her eyes while lifting my elbows towards the ceiling. Then, she places them back on the floor.

It's as if I resemble the wings of a turkey being lifted when sitting on the counter ready to stuff. Following the elbow lift, Maria presses her palms gently on my chest cavity to push air out. Her slow, but deliberate rhythmic motion of lifting and compression, as she hovers over my body, becomes more demanding for her with every breath. She continues til she brings herself to complete physical exhaustion. I open my eyes slightly to notice water droplets forming on her forehead before I shut them quickly.

"Breathe in the breath of life," she beckons.

I recognize those words of biblical origin. Internally, humming hymnal lyrics from memory, I begin to sing it silently as it plays joyfully through my head.

Breathe on me, Breath of God,
Fill me with life anew,
That I may love what Thou dost love,
And do what Thou wouldst do.

Swirling in a realm of spirituality, believing God's within me at this moment, I'm moved and think to myself,

"Am I'm being healed this very moment?"

After awhile, Maria sits back on her heels. She collects my right hand and slowly brings me back into an upright position on the floor. Arising, as if from a trance, I can't help but think,

"Am I healed? Do I feel any different?"

Maria then wipes away the moisture from her brow and face with a handkerchief; her clothing is dampened beneath her underarms. Perspiring, she appears as if she had just finished a marathon. Bringing herself back to composure, in a soft, gentle voice, she speaks to me,

"I've just received a vision."

She pauses until she has my full attention.

"In you, I see a book, a page flipping back and forth." She pauses again. "Does that mean anything to you?"

"Hum . . . ," I think to myself.

"Flipping . . . like I can't decide one way or another?"

Without denying or confirming, Maria questions further,

"How does this apply to where you are currently?"

What pops into my head startles me. Am I being faced with the question,

"Do I want to live or die?"

It hits me.

"Yes, that's it!"

Her vision directs me toward a crossroads. God's asking me to make a conscious choice. Do I take a path to pursue life or do I submissively give up? I've been told by top oncologists my cancer could take a turn either way. Maria didn't require a verbal answer, so I keep my thoughts to myself. The session ends.

Such an unusual experience leaves me curiously wondering,

"What was that all about?"

Maria's method, much like the Greek philosopher Socrates, poses more questions than answers. My rhythmic breathing, like chanting, made me light-headed, yet, somehow, I'm fully refreshed. I'm anxious to call Carol as soon as I get to the car.

"Hey Carol, I just finished my session with Maria."

"How was it?"

"Different than anything I've ever experienced."

"In what way?

"She had a vision of a book within me where a page is flipping back and forth. At first, I thought I was wavering in indecision, which is absolutely true, because I'm unsure if my cancer will return. But now, I believe the picture she paints is begging me to choose life or death."

Carol responds in a nonjudgmental tone,

"Hum . . . that could be!"

During my two-hour drive home, I think more about the unusual session, humming along with the radio. A familiar song draws a twinkle of a smile, gradually extending across my face, causing my heart to lift. In that moment, I joyfully announce out loud to God and the world,

"I choose life . . . I choose life!"

3rd base - fitness & nutrition

Changing into track shoes, shorts and a T-shirt, I step out the front door and run miles of bike paths designed to meander throughout the neighborhood.

Nature's influence clears my head with the fresh smell of pine trees that tower above the densely populated woods. Gray squirrels scurry about, preparing their winter provisions, capturing my attention when they rustle through the leaves. One timidly chases its tail, encircling itself into a frenzy.

Drinking in the outdoor serenity taps into my inner uncertainties, promoting one-on-one conversations with God. I run with Him on a path without end, unsure of my time on earth, but thankful for the strength to tread each day. We run with hope together, til I'm exhausted.

Philippians 4:13
I can do everything through him
who gives me strength.

a swim

The thought of diving into a pool of temperate water as winter approaches soothes my soul. A complete full-body immersion seems to shield me from the outside world, giving me a chance to focus my thoughts within. Freestyle sets me in forward motion, reaching for life's rhythmic pattern of two strokes between a quick breath of air. A flutter kick propels me though the water, unleashing a therapeutic power my body craves. For me, swimming provides a relaxing form of exercise while doubling as a test of endurance.

"Hum, this whole cancer process tests my physical stamina, not to mention the emotional and intellectual aspects."

I've set my compass to point toward positive energy, positive attitude and positive thoughts. I'm alive and cheerfully grateful for every chance to work out.

nutrients

Scanning through bookshelves at Barnes and Noble, I search for cookbooks and nutritional guides on how to guard against cancer. Thumbing through a few, I see recommendations to indulge in antioxidant-rich foods like blueberries, beans, and spices to ward off the disease. Further advice suggests I avoid stimulants like coffee, bacon and chocolate.

"Chocolate?"

Chocolate milk was the only milk I could stomach growing up. Hershey bars, almond joys, and pecan caramel turtles are my absolute favorites, too!

"Hum, I don't know if I can eliminate those!"

Not finding an exact list of foods as a guide, I go home empty- handed. That very day, I'm greeted with a package that reads, *Giant Book of Kitchen Counter Cures*, subtitled *117 foods that fight cancer and other health problems*. It's from my dear, former mother-in-law who resides in California.

Quite the cook herself, Frances single-handedly ran a lunch counter near the U. S. Steel plant in Joliet, a Chicago suburb, in her 30s. Elated with her find, as if we were on the same wavelength, I flip through the pages, eying some great recipes.

"This is great!"

Frances continues to hold a candle for me even though it's been six years since I parted ways with her son. This perfect guide, complete with 111 healing recipes, is signed on the inside cover with . . .

To my special, precious, beautiful, daughter Marilyn,
Your other Mother, with much Love, Frances M. Sobwick

Since meeting her, she's always been a mother to me. Her love of cooking and thoughtful gift of hope keeps me on track. While perusing the recipes, I jot down a list of ingredients and head to the store.

herbs

To further boost my immune system, I make contact with a local herbalist recommended by a friend. Since ancient cultures have practiced the study of herbs for thousands of years, identifying herbs and preparing tinctures to help different types of ailments, this alternative resource is worth investigating.

Entering the herbalist's dark but cozy office space, my curiosity is drawn to her shelves lined with a variety of capsuled potions meant to offer affective healing properties. She's prepared packets customized to build up my immune system. Big capsules, small capsules, big tablets, small tablets are all sorted in a rainbow of colors of designated dosage.

Making another investment, I line up these naturalist-subscribed supplements on the tabletop daily. They resemble a line of soldiers ready to go into battle, upping my vitamin and mineral quotient. With handfuls taken twice a day for several weeks, I notice gaining weight in the process.

"Ah . . . not more weight gain?"

But, since health is the priority here, I forge ahead with taking the supplements.

my masseuse

Weekly appointments for a full body massage are part of my recovery regime. Bolstering my immune system with physical touch outweighs my risk of cancer cell stimulation. After all, Angie found my cancerous tumor in the first place and under her careful watch, she'd let me know if she detected any changes.

When stretched out, lying face down on a soft but firm, comfortable massage table between two flannel sheets, I hear soft zen-like melodies filling the room. It puts my mind to rest, forgetting about everything else but the present. Herb-scented oils moisten my skin with mineral molecules rubbed gently into every pore, exuding a pleasing aroma. Adding eucalyptus essential oil to jojoba oil creates a fragrant smell lightly lingering.

Her rhythmic hands apply pressure to every tissue, relieving trigger points, slowly releasing stress. Healing signals transmit up and down my spine, putting me into a trance. Muscles melt into relaxation as blood flow increases.

I easily drift off, feeling peace within, thinking, if only this treatment could extend for another hour. Angie finds her new role as my body protectorate when I rely on her professional expertise to detect any other unusual physical abnormalities. She's truly a godsend.

home plate - my growing faith

Since my diagnosis, my path to survival became as unconventional as my rare and deadly cancer. Running bases with God during my four-year journey started with one step, one at a time. First base included my oncologist appointments in Ohio, Minnesota, and New York, with the medical approach of trying the experimental drug thalidomide. I also met with the Ohio State University radiologist, ruling out radiation as an option against my cancer. Then, I consulted with OSU medical researchers to check on any possible genealogical link to the leiomyosarcoma. This mysterious disease offered no answers, leading to a series of dead ends. I moved on to a skip when discovering alternative resources, like "getting centered", to be anchored in both spirit and mind, logic and emotion, physical reality and the ethereal world. Then, I added acupuncture to correct meridians and points encouraging hormonal balance since a complete hysterectomy placed me into early menopause. I tried Reiki to channel positive energy into my body. By adding nutritional supplements to my diet, along with physical exercise, I gradually regained my energy and learned the value of endurance.

Making my way through a world of wellness challenge, home base represents my ever growing faith in God. Continuous communication with Him brings me a sense of peace and understanding knowing, full well, He's always there as my constant companion.

As each year passes, I touch third base realizing I have a chance to head for home. Then, I run. My heart pumps louder and louder as adrenaline rush's through me like being chased by a grizzly bear. In the summer of my fourth year after surgery, results of my final CT scan reports I'm *free and clear* of cancer. Those words, *free and clear*, echo in my head creating a state of euphoria. I'm in awe. *"Covering my Bases"* is coming to fruition. I've stepped on 1st, 2nd, and 3rd base seeking a cure for cancer over the last four years. Elated with the thought of regaining a new lease on life, my imaginary body stretches to reach home. Flying in face first, I slide into home plate. And yeah, it feels awesome. It's epic!

A HOME RUN!

How do you think of God?

Given to me during my bout with cancer,
this poetic message filled my heart with joy.

How Do You Think Of God?

*At first, I saw God as my observer, my judge, keeping
track of the things I did wrong, so as to know whether
I merited heaven or hell when I die. He was out there,
sort of like the President. I recognized His picture
when I saw it, but I didn't really know Him.*

*But later on, when I recognized my higher power, it
seemed as though life was rather like a bike ride, but
it was a tandem bike, and I noticed that God was
in the back, helping me pedal.*

*I don't know just when it was that He suggested we
change places, but life has not been the same since
- life with my higher power, that is. God makes life exciting!*

*When I had control, I knew the way. It was rather boring
but predictable. It was the shortest distance
between two points.*

*But when He took the lead, He knew delightful long cuts,
up mountains, and through rocky places at breakneck speeds.
It was all I could do to hang on! Even though it looked
like madness, He said, "Pedal!"*

*I worried and was anxious and asked, "Where are
you taking me?" He laughed and didn't answer,
and I started to learn to trust.*

*I forgot my boring life and entered into the adventure.
And when I'd say, "I'm scared," He'd lean back
and touch my hand.*

*He took me to people with gifts that I needed, gifts
of healing, acceptance and joy. They gave me their
gifts to take on my journey, our journey, God's and mine.*

*And, we were off again. He said, "Give the gifts away;
they're extra baggage, too much weight." So I did,
to the people we met, and I found that in giving, I received,
and still our burden was light.*

*I did not trust Him at first, in control of my life.
I thought He'd wreck it, but He knows bike secrets.
He knows how to make it bend, to take sharp corners,
jump to clear, high rocks, fly to shorten
scary passages.*

*And, I am learning to shut up and pedal in the
strangest places, and I'm beginning to enjoy the view
and the cool breeze on my face with my delightful
constant companion, my higher power.
And, when I'm sure I just can't do any more,
He just smiles
and says . . . "Pedal."*

Anonymous

Expedition Detour - 48 years old

Short gasps announce the urgency of my current condition but, it doesn't sink in. Slouched in disbelief, I'm acutely aware my vitality now diminished is replaced by fatigue. Every passing moment becomes vitally precious. Struggling to wrap my head around this precarious situation, I bare a blank stare that wipes plainly across my face.

Witness to my forlorn expression of hopelessness, the astute advisor prudently tells me a story of two divers faced with similar circumstances. Like an instant replay, his conclusive words ring clear. He says,

"One diver makes the decision to operate immediately on the boat and lives, while the other diver waits to get to shore for a medical incision and dies."

My mind wanders briefly, then it hits me.

"Whoa!" Is this for real? Taken aback, words form on my tongue to articulate.

"I need to make a call to my expedition leader."

Slowly, I rise from the chair managing my way to the dark alcove in search of my Filipino escort.

"We need to call Alan."

Without another word, she understands. Thankfully, she speaks fluent English. As unreliable as cell phones are in 2001 with few receiving towers, she attempts to reach Alan in Mabini Batangas. Near an outside wall where daylight peeks through, the young Philippine girl keys in the cell number of my expedition leader an hour away. Her index finger goes up to let me know she's made the connection while at the same time she walks towards me to hand over the phone.

"Hello, Hello?"

Then suddenly, the phone goes dead. Beads of moisture collect on my temples and roll down the side of my face. Inherently aware of my dire need for a decision, I wipe the wet from my brow. Every second wasted weighs heavily on my mind. Once again, I fall back against the cool smooth cement wall sliding down to the floor.

My head lowers.

"What if I can't talk to Alan?"

Losing ground quickly, I'm physically and mentally spent. Turning to God, I ask silently,

"What should I do?"

Minutes later, she tries the connection again near the outer wall. Waving her other hand, she motions another Filipino to help me stand up and walk over to reach her, not to jeopardize the signal. Recognizing my expedition leader's voice, I blurt out quickly.

"I have an 80% collapsed lung and they need to operate. Should I go to Manila?"

Knowing Manila to be the only city in the Philippines with the most advanced medical facility, he replies,

"Yes, go to Manila."

Followed by dead silence, the call drops again. Beads of water droplets run down my back as I gasp for another breath.

"How would I get to Manila?"

a week earlier

A sharp pain pierces my chest, causing my body to flinch forward as I place the palm of my hand over my heart. Searching for a seat, I wait for the pain to subside to catch my breath before I resume packing for another Earthwatch dive expedition.

It occurs to me, I've had this kind of pain at least once before. Ah.., it's pleurisy. I recall now. Liquid collecting around my lung tissue initiates inflammation creating shortness of breath. Last week's head cold moved down into my lungs instigating this sharp stabbing chest pain. Ugh!

My timing couldn't be worse since my scheduled flight to the Philippines leaves tomorrow. Sitting upright helps to avoid painful chest discomfort. By propping up a pile of pillows behind my back and neck, raised up as if I'm lying on a mountainside, I can breathe comfortably. This is the only way I can get a restful night's sleep before I pack a bottle of ibuprofen and fly overseas as planned.

Making a stop in Hong Kong for a week gives my sore, inflamed lung recovery time prior to scuba diving in Luzon, the largest island of the Philippines. Touring Hong Kong preoccupies my mind as I climb 260 stone steps leading to Big Buddha, perched high atop Lantau Island Hill.

At the summit, I'm completely mesmerized by colossal structures serving this city's massive population. I see hundreds of skyscrapers filled with apartments, office space, restaurants and shopping centers, creating the vertical-structured landscape from atop Hong Kong's island peak.

From sipping afternoon tea and sampling finger sandwiches at the very famous posh Peninsula Hotel to walking through city street wet markets, open fresh-air live fish shops, I'm truly surrounded by a vast, rich cultural diversity. As an active tourist consumed with the sights and sounds of Hong Kong, I continue to swallow ibuprofen to reduce inflammation surrounding my lung in preparation for diving.

By weeks end, my flight nears touch-down in Manila, where I peer out my window at miles of underdeveloped landscape. Poorly constructed buildings dotting the surface represent the living and working conditions of over 25 million impoverished Philippine people. The meager existence below contrasts our privileged lifestyle stateside.

After one night's rest in Manila, our expedition team meets and loads into a van for a four-hour drive heading south to the remote destination of Mabini Batangas, a coastal village.

Swarms of cars, trucks, jeepneys and mopeds fill the already overcrowded streets where local drivers are oblivious to any kind of driving etiquette. Crammed roadways with bumper-to-bumper traffic give way to child beggars tapping on our windows for handouts.

A constant cacophony of honking and disorder make navigating through the streets unnerving, causing utter chaos in all directions. Safely sheltered inside our van, we make our way to the outskirts of town. The highway pavement turns to gravel roads, and, the gravel roads turn to dirt, leaving a cloud of dust behind us in the baking sun.

It's not long before civilized conveniences like gas stations leave our sight. I keep my fingers crossed that the engine will not overheat. If a tire goes flat, being stranded under this scorching sun is like being in a desert without water. Our wheels keep rolling til finally, hours later, our van creeps its way down the steep coastal cliff to our expedition base camp by dusk.

mabini batangas

The small Philippine dive resort nestled at the bottom of a hillside near inlet ocean waters accommodates our dive team in tight-knit quarters. We pair up into small, open-air thatched huts housing two single mattresses, two cots and little green geckos. Even in April, steamy temperatures hang throughout nightfall as we unpack for our practice dive with our new dive buddy tomorrow morning.

At sunup, we methodically reel out our transect lines along the coastal reef, approximately 25-30 feet below the surface. Each end must be carefully secured by looping the line gently around a piece of hard coral without causing harm to the stationary formation. We hold our waterproof checklist in one hand, freeing our other for writing or hand signal communications.

Incrementally, coral types found beneath and along the

transect line are checked off. Coordinating tasks with our dive buddy becomes routine when completing our mission. Collecting data efficiently proves critical, considering we must keep an eye on water pressure and time allowed underwater for safe diving.

So far, our initial test run moves along perfectly until we resurface. Extending each arm forward, I gasp for air, swimming to shore. My ankles feel as if weights were attached, pulling me down beneath the water while my arms grow heavier with each stroke. Grabbing my mouthpiece, I suck in air, kicking feverishly to reach shallow waters. I struggle like a hooked fish at the end of a fishing line til finally, my fins touch bottom. Stooping down to remove my fins, I leave my dive boots on to walk on shore. Every footstep feels unsteady when hauling my heavy, cumbersome air tank, causing my knees to quiver.

"Why am I feeling so weak?"

Normally, I'd feel refreshed and re-energized following an early swim in the ocean, but this morning was different. After a rainwater rinse under an outdoor spigot and quick change into shorts and a T-shirt, it's lunchtime. Still quite out of breath, I trek up forty flagstone steps to the dining patio where fellow divers rendezvous. Reaching the top step leaves me looking peaked and lightheaded, drawing my expedition leader's attention.

"Marilyn, you look pale. Are you feeling all right?"

Suddenly the world around me moves in circular motion. Reaching for a chair, I sit down to get my bearings while saying in reply,

"I've been taking ibuprofen this past week to clear up pleurisy, but, I may need something stronger."

"Maybe you should go to the clinic in Batangas City. It's an hour's drive from here."

"An hour?"

"Yes, Bryan was there just last week to get some medication."

Bryan, another dive volunteer, arrived a week earlier than the rest of the dive team. I knew him from a previous expedition.

Considering the physical demands of a diver, I'll need some medication with ten days of diving ahead of me. My partner relies on me. A pharmacy doesn't even exist near this remote coastal camp, so, the facility an hour away is my only viable resource since I'll need something stronger than aspirin!

"There's a drug store near the clinic," says Alan, our expedition research leader.

"Okay, I'll go."

I don't mind taking the advice of a highly-admired marine geologist and founder/president of the Coastal Conservation and Education Foundation. He knows the area quite well, having organized dive teams to collect data in Philippine waters supporting his research program entitled *Saving Philippine Reefs*. His wife Vangie is Filipino. Together they have a son named Ion. While they reside in Hawaii, they have a second coastal home a short distance from our dive site here in Mabini Batangas.

batangas city

Our coastal setting, though beautiful for exploring coral reefs, is completely removed from civilization. A couple of locals, hired to help with our expedition, drive me to the clinic in Batangas City. In the van, we climb up the steep, clay-covered roads from our dive resort, dodging huge gullies created from spring's torrential rains.

Fissures look to be a foot deep, making the van tilt back and forth as we hobble up the hill like a car on the rails of an amusement park roller coaster ride. Along the way, livestock randomly cross our path at their own pace, testing our patience as we wait for those scrawny-looking cattle to move aside.

Feeling a bit impatient after catching my breath in the back seat, I wonder whether we'll even get to the clinic at this pace. Peering out my side window, I see an overabundance of political posters littering the open terrain along our route with paper strewn everywhere within view. Natural habitat has little chance of escaping trash left scattered about the sun-drenched dry and dusty territory.

Approaching city limits, oncoming vehicles head straight for us. And, like a game of chicken, drivers bully one another, competing for the right of way. Honks surge from both vehicles as we squeeze past one another with only inches to spare on either side of our van. Commotion outside the van creates uneasiness within me as I take in another noticeable, deep breath of air.

Closer to town, I see a mother walking with her young son along the dusty road, holding an umbrella to shield them both from the afternoon's blazing sun. Vertical waves of steamy heat visible to the naked eye rise beneath their feet.

Sixty minutes seems like eternity by the time we reach the medical facility. Making our way up the entrance steps, our iris aperture adjusts to navigate the dark corridor of cement floors and walls. Natural light is the only source of illumination for this building during the midday heat.

Filipinos form a line ahead of me, awaiting medical attention as my native escort motions me to sit on a cement platform along the wall. She slithers ahead of the queue. It's obvious I'm the only Caucasian in the corridor. Either my condition or skin color creates a noticeable parting of the crowd because, a few moments later, she comes back to shuffle me forward to a room the size of a closet to meet a young Filipino, said to be a medical advisor. After a brief introduction, we sit down face-to-face and he says,

"Describe your symptoms."

"I've had shortness of breath today, but the day before I left the states, I had pleurisy. That was a week ago. I've been taking aspirin to reduce the inflammation since then."

He listens attentively and replies,

"I suggest we take some X-rays to see what's going on."

Following his lead, while catching my breath, we walk down the dark gloomy corridor into a room housed with large antiquated-looking equipment on wheels. Under my breath

I mutter with discontent,

"Bet these emit tons of radiation!"

The heat of the day finds its way into the dimly-lit room. High humidity levels saturate the air, making it even heavier to breathe. Teenage-looking medical facility assistants fumble around, taking exposures while I envision high-speed electrons bombarding me.

Their awkward handling of X-ray equipment, in addition to whispering to one another, raises my doubts about their capabilities. None of them look confident when adjusting and re-adjusting the dials to capture proper X-rays. All the while, I think to myself, how spoiled am I by advanced western medical facilities. Secretly, I wish I could be back in the states right now. Finishing their task, they ask me to stand outside down the hall to wait for the X-rays to be processed. Several minutes go by until the doc approaches me, clearing his throat.

"The films didn't develop properly. We'll need to take more exposures."

Not surprised, I begrudgingly repeat gestures, lifting my arms above my head for the next set of chest X-rays. Exasperated by this process, my body starts to collapse, causing me to quickly grasp the edge of a solid cement-block platform. Pulling myself up, I lift my hip to the edge and recline into a fetal position. Totally spent, all energy leaves my body; my eyes close.

I rest my cheek peacefully against the smooth, cool surface while lying on my side. Oh . . . it feels calming just to rest here awhile. Unable to move, I hear attendants whisper, not knowing how to deal with me lying on their only X-ray table in the middle of the room. Calling for more assistance, collectively they decide to lift my body and usher me back down the hall. Steadied in a standing position, propped against the cool cement wall, I lean back, sliding down to the cement floor.

In the absence of waiting rooms or chairs for patients, dark, cavernous hallways serve as my place of refuge until I receive further word. Slivers of daylight peek in around the corner wall, visually suggesting my immediate area of privacy. Only the sound of my labored breathing is amplified against cement surfaces.

Growing weaker, I await results of the second round of X-rays. I'm motioned back to the medical advisor's office. Placing the palm of my hand against the wall to assist myself to stand erectly, I walk slowly forward to discuss his findings. He clamps the films to the back light 18 by 24 inch display screen on the wall and says,

"Your right lung . . ," pointing to the film, "is a good example of what a normal lung looks like. Over here is your left lung."

My eyes focus on a dark kidney shape sitting on the bottom of my chest cavity.

"So," I say, "what does that mean?"

"It means you have an 80% collapsed lung. Your lung is that dark, deflated sac."

Bewildered by his findings, I understand this is way beyond pleurisy. The advisor says,

"We'll need to operate."

"Operate!"

Stunned, I'm frozen stiff in my chair. My mind races to

retrace the origin of my current condition, reviewing my morning dive. Staring at the tiny dark kidney-shaped sac on the small screen in front of me is a visual reminder of this newly discovered predicament. I concede, an aspirin quick fix is no longer an option.

back to operate

Uniquely aware of my fragile condition, the Philippine medical advisor walks into the hall, escorting me back into his small office. He pulls up a chair motioning me to sit down and he adjusts another seat next to mine. I begin to reiterate,

"My expedition leader suggests I go to Manila for the operation."

The young advisor turns his head slowly, pauses, and looks directly into my eyes before he answers,

"I could get you transportation to Manila, but it would be at least a three-hour drive, depending on traffic. You know how unpredictable that can be with your journey down the coast."

Witness to my blank expression, he carefully carries on,

"With your lung currently 80% collapsed after this morning's dive, each breath you take inflates your chest cavity. It's just a matter of time before your heart shuts down. At the very most, you might have three hours left."

My head drops to my chest. Trying to clear my thoughts, I desperately try to sort out this day.

"How could a morning dive lead to less than three hours to

live? I repeat to myself, less than three hours? Less than 3 hours!"

Dumbstruck, shocked, I raise my chin, penetrating the pupils of his dark brown eyes while gently closing my fingers around his forearm searching for an answer. Looking straight at him I ask,

"Can you help me?"

"Yes! I can operate, here."

Inside myself, I'm increasingly aware that I'm growing weaker. My eyes become filled with uncertainty. Reading my body language, the advisor continues patiently,

"The procedure is simple. To allow the trapped air to escape, we poke a small hole in your chest cavity by your rib cage here." He points to my side.

"If we don't give the air building up inside an escape route, your chest will expand like a balloon, putting pressure on your heart, forcing it to shut down."

Stuck between a rock and a hard spot, I can't rationalize further. The clock's ticking; I've got to decide. Clearing a path for immediate action, the advisor suggests,

"I can call in an anesthesiologist and prepare surgical papers for signing."

I'm acutely aware that my body feels a dramatic change since the short time I walked into this facility, so, I say,

"Okay."

Still seated, I quiet myself in silent prayer with God to make certain of my decision. Feeling too weak to second-guess, I sign the papers with little time to spare.

time's running out

A rickety, rusty wheelchair carries me up a V-configured cement ramp to the 2nd floor; this basic-constructed facility is without modern-convenience elevators. My squeaky chair rattles back and forth as I'm being pushed up the ramp into surgery. It hasn't seen a can of WD-40 in awhile!

Once we are inside this dark, sparsely-appointed room, a clinic attendant finishes preparing surgical knives and other utensils to rest neatly on a white cloth supported by a small, portable tray table. A single light bulb hangs above another cement platform in the middle of this room with windowless walls. Left alone in this quiet, eerie space, I look around. Questions bombard me rapidly in succession.

"Are these operating instruments sanitized? Is a Philippine advisor and his local Filipino anesthesiologist qualified for this surgical procedure? Why were American missionaries, recently reported in world news, killed here in the Philippines? And why, God, father of my very existence, am I face-to-face with death again? What is it? What am I not getting? Have I not lived up to your expectations?"

My mind races as I speed through my personal checklist,

"No spouse,

No children,

No debts,

No unfinished business,

My earthly existence is a wrap!

My housekeeping list is complete!

Okay, I get it.

My work on earth is done, period."

When under the gun, it didn't take long to sum up my life, realizing I'm expendable. With that thought behind me, I praise God, thanking him for my great childhood, for my loving family, whose strong characteristics carried us though life's challenges. Our characteristics, woven together, include Dad's eternal optimism, Mom's resourcefulness, my sister Pat's enthusiasm, and my sister Carol's gift of song. As for me, the creative middle daughter, I do my best to bridge any gaps that may arise between us.

As I'm returning from my private thoughts, the medical advisor enters the room with the anesthesiologist and a couple of female assistants. He introduces the team. While making procedure preparations, he asks me,

"Could you step out of the wheelchair and recline on this platform with your left hip up? That way, I can gain access to your chest wall."

"Yes," thinking to myself,

"Is this DIY, do it yourself, surgery? Maybe he'll ask me to make the incision too!"

Western medical practices have definitely spoiled me, but I'm not in Kansas anymore! Nor is this the land of OZ! As I'm in position with my left hip up, an IV catheter is inserted, administering a knockout drug. While I scan the room for the last time, the team positions themselves around me. Nervously,

I convey to the staff,

"I'm with Earthwatch Organization to help our world."

Pressed for time, I struggle to say something meaningful to gain their sympathy,

"I'm grateful to you all."

Then, with a brief pause as I catch my next breath, my voice inflects words of encouragement,

"Good Luck!"

Like a ticker tape, last minute thoughts run through my mind,

"Are we all on the same team? Will I regain consciousness? Is this the end of my life on earth?"

Fading quickly, I silently call out to God,

"I'm in your hands."

Meanwhile, my expedition leader, an hour away, my family and friends, half a world away, have no idea I'm undergoing emergency surgery, fighting for my life.

a whale of a blowhole

By the sound of a soft-humming window air conditioner, my eyes open in unfamiliar surroundings. A blurred figure, outlined by soft beams of light that radiate from her silhouette, is standing at the foot of my bed. Trying to focus, I ask myself,

"Am I dreaming? Is this heaven?"

Her body shape begins to move about the space. Moments later, another figure enters the room, moving towards me, collecting my hand.

"Your surgery went well," says the Filipino advisor.

A fog drifts through my head, assimilating this gentle voice. Searching for memory of where I am, within myself I hear the words,

"I'm alive, I'm alive!"

Feeling utterly elated about returning to this world, I ly quietly, listening intently as the medical advisor briefs me,

"I've sent word to your expedition team and notified DAN, Divers Alert Network, about your successful surgery. Your team leader, Alan White, is driving up tomorrow morning to see you."

I'm feeling weak but comforted with his reassuring news. He goes on to describe details of my surgery, a story he felt would confirm that I'd made the right decision. He offers more details,

"At point of insertion, air spewed out of you like a whale blow hole. Poof! Swoosh!, nearly knocking me over."

Thinking to myself,

"WOW, I just dodged another bullet! That means I must have been down to my last hour on earth. I'm imagining the scene in the operating room,

"There she blows! If only they had a video of the procedure."

Gently lifting a tube attached to my left rib cage, he points out the surgical incision leading to my lung. Under my breath I'm saying to myself, "Guess I'll be connected to my bedside apparatus at least through the night."

"We've attached a liquid collection bag to monitor your CC levels (fluid collection). We'll need to take more X-rays right away to ensure your lung is re-inflated."

I thought to myself,

"Oh great, more radiation!" He says,

"We can do this while you're lying here."

After he leaves, attendants wheel in portable X-ray equipment and place a couple of radiation shield blankets on either side of my lung. I lay quietly, no longer needing to gasp for air. In a short time, I receive word that my lungs are fully re-inflated, putting my emergency situation to rest. Exhausted from surgery at the end of this traumatic day, I slowly doze off.

I'm awakened by the morning sun faintly lighting my room directly in front of me, as a nurse carefully arranges a tray of pills, presenting them to me bedside. Hesitant to imbibe, I inquire,

"What are these?"

She rattles off pharmaceutical names sounding like gibberish, but I don't have a clue regarding their chemical compounds. I figure if they intended to kill me, I'd be dead by now. Receiving a cup of water handed to me, I swallow them with a prayer that it's truly medicine.

A soft ring . . . ring . . . filters through the room, coming from a phone sitting on the desk at the foot of my bed. The attendant answers on the second ring and speaks softly into the mouthpiece, nodding while collecting a long extension cord, then handing me the receiver,

"Hello?" I say.

"Good Morning. I'm your DAN representative."

Even as a member of DAN, Divers Alert Network, a divers insurance organization, I didn't expect to hear from them. The caller asks,

"How are you?"

"I've survived surgery," which I'm proud to say.

"We've been notified by the Philippine medical facility concerning your pneumothorax yesterday as the result of a diving accident."

"Yes, that would be me."

"We've located your whereabouts. Being in Bantangas City, a small industrial port, you're in a region of potentially high political danger."

"Oh?"

"Yes, ... to air flight you back to the U. S. is too risky for us. The process of moving you out of the area would attract unwanted attention."

Most divers, like myself, subscribe to DAN without ever guessing we'd actually need medical assistance. Hmm . . . what does he mean, a politically dangerous area?

"We'll check back with you again tomorrow. Bye."

"Goodbye."

Wasn't that a brief how-de-do! Connected to a tube protruding from my rib cage and weary from painkillers, I didn't feel up to making demands. If I could just get more sleep, maybe I'll feel better. At least now, I know someone in the outside world is aware of my existence and my surrounding circumstances.

Neatly tucked under sheets in a hospital bed, I think about getting back to my expedition campsite in Mabini Batangas. In my make-believe mind, I picture night mechanics working on me full-time, fixing my body parts so I'd wake up completely healed.

Horribly disappointing to learn and overwhelmingly sad for me, my collapsed lung injury means I'll never be able to scuba dive again. To not be part of the underwater world as an expedition diver or sport diver is even more difficult to bear than going through an emergency surgery. Rather than drown in my sorrows, I reminisce about earlier dives, feeling grateful.

Throughout the day, as I'm fading in and out of sleep, flashbacks of diving so many clear, tropical water dive sites recall one instance in the Bahamas of a big-lip grouper, AKA the local Casanova. Slowly approaching in big grouper fashion, he lays a big smooch on my dive mask. Unfazed by scuba divers entering his space, he acts confidently as an ambassador amid his sea life kingdom, welcoming divers with a kiss. He brings a smile to my face at the thought of his smug, affectionate action towards divers.

- In Barbados, I'm witness to sea life personalities when studying mating habits of damselfish. Committed to their ocean water column, feisty little male damsels protect and defend female eggs freshly laid under a sheltered canopy. Males dance and bully natural sea life threats, creating distraction to keep predators away from the nest they're guarding. Characteristic of a human behavior, a male damsel paces furiously back and forth in front of his post, while yet another "Mr. Leisure" slowly patrols with a watchful eye.

- Effortlessly kicking my fins to swim alongside green

and loggerhead turtles in the Florida Keys, I can't help but marvel at their ocean water navigation skills. Their internal GPS, global positioning system, never fails. And to think those globetrotters visit several continents annually without a passport!

- On the ocean floor near Cayman Brac, we kneel down on the sandy bottom to catch a peek of green moray eels quickly swerving in and out of coral structures like snakes. They're playful, slippery, sleek and sneaky when foraging for their next meal. When their mouths expand like a stretched rubber band, they appear exceedingly ferocious to unsuspecting prey.

- In Stingray City surrounding Cayman Islands, my fingertips lightly touch the soft, silky, white underbellies of stingrays who soar gracefully through waters overhead. Smooth to the touch, their undersides reveal a duel set of breathing vents positioned like runway lights flapping open and closed. Those vents, like a vacuum, suck in the hair on my head as they swoop in closely overhead, seeking fish handouts from divers.

- Camouflaged on a sandy ocean floor in Bonaire, a peacock flounder burrows to protect itself from predators until a nearby disturbance causes it to scurry to another place of refuge. I'm delightfully surprised to see its fins flutter along the ocean floor, moving in all directions since their eyes sit atop their head like a radar dish. They're flat as a pancake and shaped like a platter, hovering gracefully to dissuade attention. Then, it burrows itself again in the sandy bottom, changing color externally in eight seconds to blend into its surroundings.

- In the Cayman Islands, carrying an underwater camera with

a macro lens, I steady myself above tiny Christmas tree worms that suddenly collapse like upside down umbrellas when the slightest water disturbance rushes past their tiny limbs. It becomes a test of patience, waiting til these delicate specimens dare open their cone-shaped branches to feed on plankton. Only then can I press the camera button, capturing a perfect photographic, underwater, Christmas-tree image.

- I remember quick-witted dolphins in Bahamian waters, flaunting their expert swimming skills, responding to my hand signals, creating our one-on-one connection. Eager to interact with these intelligent mammals, trainers teach us how to use our body language to exchange signals. With my arms outstretched while I'm standing on the ocean floor, a dolphin moves toward me in a rush with a modest swish of its tail fin. My heartbeat accelerates in anticipation of being its under-water playmate. Keeping my body stiff while its rostrum gently meets the palm of my hand, it turns me around 360 degrees. Magically engaged, I feel like a ballerina in a water wonderland.

- Near Grand Bahama Island, thirty feet down to the ocean floor, I meet black slit eyes, like that of a cat, belonging to the mysterious reef sharks. Their deadly stares lack warmth or compassion as they hunt to keep sea life population in balance. Like watchdogs, they prowl the ocean, appearing hauntingly unmistakable. As observing divers, we kneel shoulder-to-shoulder on the sandy bottom, transmitting a large sonar, tricking the sharks into thinking we're bigger. I feel an awesome sense of courage, sharing underwater space with them.

- In Bermuda, during the heat of the day, shiny silver barracudas reflect the sun's light just below the surface. Their sleek, lean bodies move in sync with surrounding current, glistening like tinsel on a Christmas tree. I can't help but stare directly back at them, being cautious not to pose a threat as they pass by.

- Off the coast of Belize, frenzied movements tucked within tiny coral cubicles bring me in for a closer look at lobster tentacles skirmishing about. Like fencing with their miniature swords they stare straight towards me with their beady, pinhead eyes. Seeing them so vulnerable, I can only envision them as succulent, tender, white chunks of fresh shellfish dipped in warm melted butter, ready to devour. How easy it would be to scoop up several of these mouthwatering crustaceans, so neatly stashed in the coral wall.

- Exploring shipwrecks is creepy when swimming through the galley doors of their crusty remains. Still recognizable, the hull of a ship sits peacefully on the ocean floor, providing protected shelter areas for spawning. In the Caymans, the Oro Verde shipwreck is the artificial reef, home to countless colorful tropical fish. Rusted metal, as a result of salty water, leaves stains on my wet suit when I squeeze through too closely. Through openings of yet another wreck in Bermuda off of the Carolina coastline, I'm pushed into the hull by a strong underwater sea surge. I kick forward to separate myself from the wreckage without making any headway in the strong current. I change directions to escape.

- One last thought given to memory are tiny little "Nemos" hiding in soft, gracefully swaying, pastel-colored sea anemones found in the Philippine waters. Those crafty clown fish dress in bright orange and white stripes, challenging me to quickly snap a shot of them before they disappear behind those stinging tentacle clusters, the soft finger-like anemones. A game of peekaboo characterizes their distinctive behavior with observers.

Hour after hour, lying in bed recovering, I reminisce about those hidden treasures of the oceans, keeping those memories close to my heart. I gratefully bask in thoughts of those awe-inspiring dive experiences, feeling gratitude.

"Thank you, God, for allowing me to share the wonder and delight of your magnificent marine life creatures."

a day later

Being kept a secret in this Philippine medical center, my 24/7 -supervised room is under lock and key. I think to myself,

"Could threatening, local political terrorists be looking for ways to cause disturbance, compromising my safety in this facility? Would radicals bust through the door, waving guns and threatening to kill an American if their demands weren't met? Could I, an American volunteer scuba diver, be enough to claim ransom?"

Completely removed from what's familiar in this seaport village of political unrest, I lay clueless without access to the outside world. I'm feeling a bit uneasy.

a red dye

It's day three at Saint Patrick's Medical facility, the same place I arrived to purchase aspirin and where I'm now hospitalized. Today, I learn my Philippine advisor received his medical training to become a doctor in Canada. Relieved by the news and feeling much better about my care, my medical advisor, AKA Dr. Perez, walks in, saying,

"How are you feeling?"

"So much better, thanks to you and your staff."

"I can tell. Considering your progress, I suggest we do a medical procedure called a pleurodesis."

"A what?"

"A pleurodesis plugs any possible leaks. To ensure your lungs don't collapse again on your flight back to the states, we inject a red dye to coat the lung surface."

"Like a super glue?"

"Yes, in a way," Dr. Perez goes on to say. "It's a preventative measure. My Canadian medical training considers it normal procedure, although it's not currently practiced in the U. S."

"Then, is it necessary?"

"To avoid recurrence of another pneumothorax, I'd recommend it. We'll shoot die through your existing, attached plastic tube already in place."

Since Dr. Perez, AKA Filipino medical advisor, pulled me through emergency surgery, saving my life, I trust he'll guide me to recovery.

"If it's what you recommend, then, yes."

Having learned Dr. Perez is a Canadian trained MD clears a path for confidence in taking the next step. His personally trained staff surrounds me with the kind of reassurance I need, considering I'm half a world away from what's familiar. They've either earned my trust or I've been brainwashed!

scared and fidgety

When coming to, following the pleurodesis procedure, I'm gasping for air. Drawing in each breath causes pain in my chest. My head feels too heavy to lift from the pillow.

"Wait a minute," I ask.

"Why am I experiencing similar symptoms of labored breathing like when I first arrived here?"

Trapped under my covers, lying flat on my back, uncertainty begins to gnaw at me. Fearfully, I question,

"Where am I in this building? Where am I in Bantangas City? Am I a guinea pig? Will I ever get out? How do I navigate my way to safety? God, what's going on?"

Joshua 1:9

Have I not commanded you?
Be strong and courageous.
Do not be terrified;
do not be discouraged,
for the LORD your God will be
with you wherever you go."

Stirring within my vulnerability, my dialogue with God ensues. I linger in loneliness, erasing fears together with Him. Through an extended exchange about my situation, while still drowsy from coming out of the anesthesia, I eventually settle in His comfort as nightfall creeps in.

pee-yew!

A rank smell suddenly awakens me. Surrounded by pitch black, a pungent odor makes me nauseous with every breath I take.

"Oh . . . I'm getting sick to my stomach."

It smells like a skunk or sulfuric gas from a geyser, like Old Faithful. This foul odor of rotten eggs envelops me. I'm confined to my bed and can't move in any direction.

"Where's it coming from? Is it toxic? I'm stuck. Am I a victim of a hostile takeover?"

Nightfall makes this situation terrifying. I listen attentively, but hear nothing while lying face up. I commence conversation with God, knowing he's there.

"Is this another test?"

I beseech Him to maintain my sanity since I can't physically leave the area in my own defense. I'm a sitting duck. With further discussion, I surmise that, although the odor is in-my-face, repulsive, it may not be threatening.

"No screaming. No gunfire. All's quiet."

I release myself from worry, concluding my only escape is

nodding off.

"Olfactory glands, please shut down. I plead with myself, fall asleep, fall asleep!"

In the morning, I inquire,

"What's that foul smell?" An orderly, entering, replies,

"An elderly female patient was wheeled in while you were sleeping and she defecated."

"That confirms that!"

The unbearable stench still lingers around me as the attendants mop the floor. Even the smell of ammonia would be better.

I ask within,

"Did she die?"

I didn't have the nerve to ask out loud.

Like being on an island in my hospital bed, surrounding activity keeps me on high alert. Unpredictable and sometimes unnerving situations fall within these four walls. Anything can happen. Through it all, God remains my constant companion. We share one-on-one chats every conscious, waking hour. At age 48, I guess God thinks it's about time I did!

Psalm 23

The Lord is my shepherd;

I shall not want. He maketh me to lie down in
green pastures: he leadeth me beside the still
waters. He restoreth my soul: he leadeth me in
the paths of righteousness for his name's sake.
Yea, though I walk through the valley
of the shadow of death, I will fear no evil:
for thou art with me; thy rod and thy staff
they comfort me. Thou preparest a table
before me in the presence of mine enemies:
thou anointest my head with oil;
my cup runneth over. Surely goodness and
mercy shall follow me all the days of my life:
and I will dwell in the house of the Lord forever.

high school promise

One conversation with God takes me down memory lane, back to my junior year in high school. I'm sitting on a bench seat in the waiting room of Middlesex Hospital in New Brunswick, NJ. In solitude, I await quietly just outside the ICU, Intensive Care Unit, to say goodbye to dad, lying on the gurney on the other side of the door. He suffers from labored breathing. His lungs can't seem to clear out.

The last few nights at home, I'd hear him gasp for air, cough and wheeze from the master bedroom down the hall from me. We're now, my sisters and I, asked to say goodbye to dad as we file into his ICU space. I wonder if dad even recognizes us now that his whole body has swelled like a balloon with sausage fingers, a swollen neck, and face becoming more unrecognizable to us. He's beginning to turn blue. Returning to the waiting room, I cover my face with both hands, bow my head, close my eyes and pray intensely. I plead with God to allow dad to breathe again.

"If you save my dad, I'd commit to spreading the word. I know I'm not a preacher, but by whatever means, I'll commit to tell people about Jesus."

Philippines 4:6-7

Do not be anxious about anything, but in everything, by prayer and petition, with thanksgiving, present your requests to God. And the peace of God, which transcends all understanding, will guard your hearts and your minds in Christ Jesus.

Well, I said it. I cut a deal with God! What? Who cuts a deal with God, the Almighty?

My fervent prayer, a desperate plea for God's help, is standard procedure when I'm in dire need. For the record, I still seek God in times of stressful situations and probably always will!

After a long, restless night, not knowing dad's condition, I hear the phone ring at the crack of dawn. Mom squeals,

"Your dad's alive!"

A miracle happened! Elated with happiness, I thank God profusely, jumping for joy inside myself. Instantly, I'm reminded: I cut a deal with God. I'm indebted, honor-bound to Him to keep my word.

Newsflash. It's thirty-one years later. I'm in a Philippines hospital bed, when it hits me. My empty promise to God has yet to be fulfilled.

"Aha . . . and now I have breathing problems! Is this my wake-up call? Is time running out?"

lung gymnastics

Following the pleurodesis procedure, in walks the bedside nurse, holding a contraption. Pulling up a chair, she presents me with a face mask.

"We want you to take a deep breath to lift the white ball in this plastic tube."

"Oh?" I reply.

Lifting my head to take a better look, I notice the ball is a little smaller than a ping pong ball. Without further question, I slowly suck in as asked, filling my lungs with air to maximum capacity. I'm exerting all the strength I can muster to get the ball to lift up inside the tube. Basically, I equate this to lung gymnastics. By the second air intake, it's a contest for me to get that ball to the top of the tube. My face turns red. My lungs ache, becoming increasingly painful each time I inhale. The nurse instructs me to stay on task until I've simply run out of strength to suck in. I think to myself, I'm ready for this exercise to be over. I let her know,

"I'm glad that's over with."

Little did I know, she'd be back between my every waking hour putting me through the suck-the-ball-up-the-tube regimen.

"Ugh, it's painful!"

A new day, and I'm regaining strength. I can sit up, slide down next to my hospital bed, get my balance, and take my first steps. In lieu of a bedpan, I've earned access to the nearest flush toilet. While I'm still connected to an IV, an attendant helps me navigate through a side door across the room from my gurney. As the door opens, whoosh, a blast of steamy, humid air blazes across my face. Having been privy to a room with a window air conditioner, I'm immediately reminded of the Philippine's subtropical climate. Other sections of the medical center lacked air coolant luxury.

A narrow hall leads me past tiny cribs filled with newborns already acclimated to the humidity.

God's precious little gifts lined up next to one another beg for my attention as I pass by. I'm drawn to their tiny existence via baby babble. My Filipino aide motions me to move forward, rolling my unwieldy stand that is still connected to my rib cage. When breathing in moist air, a new stench directs me towards a tiny closet space just ahead on my right where I see a door frame without a door. The smell of urine reeks from a ceramic toilet bowl, outlined inside with a brownish-yellow water stain. While it resembles an updated flush toilet, its unkempt, unsanitary condition forces me to hold my breath, finish my business, and exit.

foreigner in clinic

Gradually, word spreads throughout St. Patrick's staff about my presence, a white patient in the hospital. One evening, when propped-up in my bed, a couple of young Filipino faces peek around the corner of my room door as my evening meal's delivered. They're anxious to have a glimpse of me, the foreigner. I catch sight of their curious eyes and lift my arm and wave. For a moment, I'm feeling like a celebrity, but at the same time, I remind myself that I'm being kept hidden for a reason.

corn in can

Asian-influenced cuisine during my stay at the clinic consists of a pile of rice for breakfast, a pile of rice for lunch, and a pile of rice for dinner, a native staple both bland and unappetizing. After my first meal of chicken broth, rice appeared regularly. Now, almost five days later, a meal cart is rolled in next to my gurney and, plated on my food tray next to my rice heap is a piece of poultry! I notice the added selection, saying,

"Chicken, yum!"

Filled with delight, I nod with appreciation. I could tell he, the food preparer, is proud to add poultry when a smile crosses his face. Feasting my eyes on rice and chicken, I fork up the combo, since my appetite's returned. He lingers to watch me consume the meal. Happily indulging, I ask him,

"Do you have vegetables, like beans or corn?"

He lights up with an understanding of the English language in quick reply.

"Oh, corn in can?"

"Yes," I reply.

The young fellow acknowledges my request and carries on with his work, waving goodbye as he walks out the door.

Knowing most Filipino households typically raise their own chickens to feed their families, I'm certain this poultry was freshly slaughtered earlier that day. I think about a typical Filipino daily meal beginning with a chicken selected from the brood. In one hand they grasp the head while the body is pulled down with the other hand until the neck pops from the spine. Bingo, the chicken's dead. Their farm to fork process is simple. Grab a fowl, yank it's head, cook, and consume!

Little did I know, the next evening, the server is proud to present me with a bowl of corn poured directly from a can served at room temperature. I'm elated. Grinning ear to ear, I spoon a mouthful of corn, acknowledging his effort, aimed to please.

"Thank-you so much!"

He nods in reply. Not only does he deliver the food tray, but he shops the local markets and prepares the meal! In this small town, working at the hospital is prestigious employment where only the most qualified locals work. The medical center's small, but efficient staff, go the extra mile to accommodate patients, a quality instilled in them.

Even though I would have liked the corn heated, I'm humbly grateful in this impoverished society. I wonder if this can of corn expense came from his own pocket. Becoming more and more aware of my immediate surroundings, I sense the gentle care I've been given during my stay. I thank God for shedding light on what it means to accept kindness and grace from those having less means to provide. Yet, all my needs are met from the most caring staff. I can't imagine that I'd be treated like such a queen anywhere else.

In the morning, the bedside attendant asks,

"Would you like your hair washed?"

Without hesitation, of course I say,

"Yes."

After two surgeries with only a gurney to call home the last 120 hours, I'm ready for some personal hygiene. Fresh-smelling hair with a bedside body wash brings me into a world beyond bedsheets and a pillow. Getting more attention from hospital staff breaks up the monotony of the day, too. She says,

"You won't need to get out of bed!"

I'm thinking silently,

"Really, does my gurney get run through a car wash?"

"I'll be behind you."

She prepares a bowl with water, collects a bottle of shampoo and creme rinse and rolls a cart behind me. Carefully lifting my head, she places a towel on the mattress and props the shallow bowl underneath my neck. Testing the tepid water with a slight touch before soaking my hair, she fills the palm of her hand with shampoo to lather into my blondish strands. Small, gentle strokes massage my scalp, practically putting me into a trance. Oh, how soothing this feels to be totally relaxed. Anxious to interact since I've been isolated so long, I exchange enjoyable conversation much like being in a hair salon. I ask,

"How long have you been here at St. Patrick's Medical Center?" She openly replies,

"I'm working here to become a registered nurse in the U. S."

Hearing her ambition to travel to America to seek her nursing degree makes me proud. Even though many countries around the world despise America, many foreigners long to become part of the land of opportunity. She says,

"Dr. Perez leads a health care program here, training nursing students in preparation for RN certification in the U. S. with the intention of us returning to the Philippines."

"Oh, that's good to hear."

As I'm her only hair washing customer today, she takes her time to ensure my comfort while I gain insight about her plans for medical training. Meanwhile, I'm grateful to be pampered.

On the next daily round, I receive welcoming news from Dr. Perez when he walks in with confidence,

"It's been seven days and it's time to remove your chest tube."

"Really? Great!"

"Would you like a painkiller while I stitch you up? It'll be a quick process."

"No thanks, I'll be fine without."

Anxious to return to the dive expedition, I decline painkillers, thinking this will speed up my release.

Pulling up a chair next to me as I sit up, the doc squeezes the tube with his forefinger and thumb, slowly withdrawing the tube from my ribcage. Closing my eyes I can't wait to finally be released from seven days of attachment. Out it comes.

"Whoo-hoo!"

Picking up the needle and thread from the tray, stitch by stitch he closes the opening in my chest wall.

"Ooooie!"

I feel the prick of the needle. Flinching with each pinch of my tender pink skin surrounding the incision, I tell myself secretly,

"Focus on freedom!"

Freedom to move about without being attached to a pole, freedom to live beyond four walls. My spirit soars with delight.

"You're done," he says.

The stitches, wiped clean with antiseptic, are covered with gauze. This great day will go down in history!

Personal belongings, including my scuba gear, fill my duffel, carried by staff to my new private hospital room on the first floor for my last night's stay. It doesn't come with air conditioning.

Open-air windows acclimate me to the humid temperatures. A solo ceiling fan is positioned directly above my new single mattress and box spring. Still under the doctor's care, my room is

James 1:2

Consider it pure joy, my brothers,
whenever you face trials of many kinds,
because you know that the testing of your
faith produces perseverance.
Let perseverance finish its work so
that you may be mature and complete,
not lacking anything.

locked until my official release. I have this new space all to myself, or so I thought.

Near dawn, while lying in bed, I reach down under my covers to itch my leg. Lifting up the sheet I discover tiny little feet have been tickling my calf. A pint-size green gecko pops his head up. Surprise! Our eyes meet. Instinctively, I jump. He makes a quick dash for the floor. For him, it's like the giant wakes up! Captivated by this curious little bedfellow, my eyes follow him around the room, up the wall, and behind a chair. At least I know he cleared my surroundings of unwanted insects. Just then, my door lock clicks with an attendant announcing,

"I've unlocked the door so you can access the bathroom."

"Thanks, that's a relief."

Now's my chance. I grab my camera, put on some street clothes, and locate the nearest exit, following natural daylight down the stairs after making a quick stop to the bathroom.

Outside the open air entry, a street vendor displays a stand-up cooler of cold drinks, an assortment of fruits, chip bags clipped together, and a pay phone sign hanging from the awning. A refreshment stand strategically placed just outside the medical center gives hospital staff and visitors amenities not found inside.

A block away stands a prominent two-story building with large bold letters that read, *City Hall*.

A menagerie of streetlights, electrical posts, and poorly maintained structures line the poorly paved road. Brightly colored political posters and banners hang randomly on vertical light posts. A tree here or bush there completes the Batangas City streetscape, where nothing is aesthetically pleasing. At last, this quick liberating walk is my first taste of freedom beyond the walls of St. Patrick's. Just to feel my leg muscles stretch and contract from memory as they did where I left off nine days ago is reassuring. Thankfully, I'm walking again. Cupped in the palm of my hand, I clutch a pocket-size camera to snatch a few area shots surrounding the clinic. I don't want to attract unwanted attention while I'm alone on the sidewalk. Within five minutes, I slip back into the facility to my single room until I'm given the go-ahead to pay my bill and be on my way.

Through the corridors and down the hall, I'm led to the billing department. Printed out on a sheet of white paper handed to me, I'm given an itemized list of services rendered. Incurred expenses include room and board, medicines, medical supplies, laboratory and X-rays, a doctor's professional fee, anesthesia, a cardiac monitor, and operating room usage fee, adding up to 89,392.24 pesos equal to $1,787.84 in U.S. dollars for a consecutive eight-night stay. And, according to U.S. standards, comparatively, a bargain. Lucky for me, MasterCard covers it!

My expedition's Philippine escorts drive up the coast to pick me up, getting me back in time to celebrate the last night with my team and to hear their adventure stories of the week. Naturally, I had one of my own!

reflections

On foreign soil where nothing's familiar I felt grateful. I'm truly grateful for the expertise and endearing kindness of the Filipino medical caregivers putting me at ease. I'm respectfully grateful for my conversations with God held with frequency, like every conscious waking moment frequency. Maybe, that's what I needed "to get", a closer relationship and total reliance on Him. Our constant exchange included the life of the Philippine people, their struggles and their triumphs. For me, a privileged American, in desperate need of their assistance, I endured a very humble life-changing experience with daily lessons on patience, understanding and thankfulness, all of which hold new meaning. During the process, my commune with God, my saving grace through it all most gratefully remains sealed within my heart.

my letter posted on
St. Patrick's Hospital web site

St. Patrick's Hospital Medical Center
Lopez Jaena St.
Batangas City, Philippines

April 22, 2001

Dear Dr. Perez and St. Patrick's Medical Staff,

Where do I begin to thank you for extending my life here on earth? Lucky for me, you came to my rescue in the nick of time. Your professional expertise and careful explanation of my nearly fatal condition offered me a guiding light. As you know, being halfway around the world from familiar surroundings added to my personal trauma. Thanks to your personal warmth and care giving, I was able to make the "Life Saving" decision.

Following your timely and skillful surgery, Dr. Perez, post-op patient care was exceptional. I would call it "Philippine Ultra Care." St. Patrick's professional staff anticipated my every need and ensured my ultimate comfort. Please extend my thanks for their kindness.

Thanks to you, Dr. Aguado, Dr. Hernandez, and nursing staff, I have survived the almost fatal diving accident.

Best of luck to you as you offer scuba divers the life-saving hyperbaric chamber and diving medical care.

Sincere thanks to all,
Marilyn Sobwick

my parents' letter, posted on
St. Patrick's Hospital website

St. Patrick's Hospital Medical Center
Lopez Jaena St.
Batangas City, Philippines

May 6, 2001

Dear Dr. Perez,

We are happy to be able to tell you that our daughter, Marilyn Sobwick, is again safely at home in Dublin, Ohio.

We live in Tulsa, Oklahoma, and as yet have not seen her. She tells us that she is fine and that it might be better to postpone a visit until she gets settled down again.

Our sole purpose in writing is to express to you our most sincere appreciation for all that you did to bring her safely through the operation. She sure was fortunate to have such a qualified person to take care of her and such a wonderful and caring staff to speed her recovery.

In each telephone call, she told us how comfortable you all made her feel and how confident she was in your ability to take care of her problem.

Again, many, many thanks and may God bless you and the hospital staff for all that you did for our daughter.

Gratefully,
Flora and Otto Seidl

epilogue

My outlook continues to be one of abiding trust and wonder as I make my way. Being caught in a sequence of catastrophic consequences, gives me proof that conducting my life without Him, simply doesn't work. My desperate call to my eternal advisor when my life was in jeopardy drew me to a defining moment. Humbled on the spot, all my previous notions of waltzing through life without Him didn't appear to show any significant meaning. My very existence was put before me.

"Who am I? What purpose do I serve?"

After my third lesson,

I asked God,

"If you need to get my attention, could it be without physical injury? I don't know if my body can take much more of this."

Thankfully, He's acknowledged my plea, because I've been given time to reflect and heal. As a result, I'm feeling more whole when we're in communication.

As the sands of time sift through an hourglass, I'll move on with certainty now that we've deepened our relationship. He knows me and I'm learning more about Him. It's like being part of His team. I'm even more comfortable about going to the next place, His heavenly kingdom.

With His assurance, I'm better equipped for the next trial.

"What will you carry in your backpack of life? Do you have an ongoing conversation with God?

"Am I ready? Are you ready?"

Scott Lengel Photography

Bio epiphany, Marilyn Seidl Sobwick

When reviewing my past, I'd tell you I've lived an ordinary life. But at age 39, I entered into a ten year span of extraordinary experiences, putting my foundation to the test.

Born in the midwest, I was brought up in a Protestant church reading Bible stories we'd freely interpret. When those biblical based beliefs were brought to trial, verses I had memorized surfaced. Those passages offered me a clear perspective in my time of need. Since then, I've begun to realize a life of purpose must be completely under the direction of one commander in chief, God.

Apparently, my first, almost fatal, accident wasn't enough to drive that message home. Then, my bout with a rare and deadly cancer didn't completely unfold God's total test of faith. It wasn't until I found myself half-way around the world that my trust in Him was brought to the next level; It's an ongoing intimate conversation with God to see me through.

Consider this an example of how God doesn't give up on even the toughest nut to crack.

Made in the USA
Middletown, DE
03 March 2025

72116824R00074